AF577401

A Gentleman Entertains

A Gentleman Entertains

A GUIDE TO
MAKING MEMORABLE
OCCASIONS HAPPEN

JOHN BRIDGES
AND
BRYAN CURTIS

THOMAS NELSON
Since 1798

NASHVILLE DALLAS MEXICO CITY RIO DE JANEIRO BEIJING

Illustrations by Alicia Adkerson, Adkerson Design

Published in Nashville, Tennessee, by Thomas Nelson
Thomas Nelson is a trademark of Thomas Nelson, Inc.

Design by Bateman Design

Library of Congress Cataloging-in-Publication Data

Bridges, John, 1950–
A gentleman entertains / John Bridges and Bryan Curtis.
p. cm.
ISBN 13: 978-1-4016-0041-9 leather
ISBN 13: 978-1-5585-3812-2 hardcase
1. Entertaining. I. Curtis, Bryan. II. Title.
TX731.B73 2000
642'.4–dc21

00–035289
CIP

Printed in the United States of America

11 12 13 14 WOR 11 10 9

For my mother

PATSY CALDWELL

for her love and her recipes.

— B. C.

For

JOE ROWLAND,

who made this book possible in ways,

I hope, only he understands.

— J. B.

Contents

Introduction

At some point in his life, every gentleman will feel the need, the pressure, or maybe even the desire, to entertain. It may be a moment when he has something to celebrate (a new job, new friends, somebody's unusually important birthday), something to hope for (maybe a new romance), or something to pay back (after a few too many weekends of letting other folks pick up the tab for the cocktails). It may even be a moment when, for no reason except his basic gentlemanliness, he has decided he just wants to be a nice guy.

When that moment arrives, however, a gentleman may discover, much to his chagrin, that his mother is nowhere to be found. He will try to remember her parties, but he may only be able to remember little sandwiches involving thinly sliced cucumbers and the sound of a whirring food processor. He will remember little bowls filled with fancy cashews. In short, it will not be exactly the kind of party he had in mind. He will look in his freezer and find nothing except a bag of ice, a box of imitation tangerine-flavored popsicles, and a couple of single-serving chicken potpies. He will glance around his living room and discover there are lint balls under the sofa. He will try not to think about the bathroom where the formerly white tile is now an odd shade of green.

There is no real reason, even at such a moment, for a gentleman to panic. Instead, it is a time for methodical planning, attention to a few details, and not sweating anything. This may be the moment, in fact, when he realizes that, just because he is a guy, he does not necessarily have to be a klutz.

He may have to realize that he is a grown gentleman now, and that it's high time he thought about planning a party. Because he is a gentleman, he can survive even the evening that bears down upon him. Better yet, he can survive it with style, by being resourceful, doing the best he can, and relying on his higher instincts.

There are signs that at least some of those instincts are worth trusting. He already has a bag of ice in the refrigerator. And, for any gentleman planning a party, that is a very good place to start.

When a gentleman entertains his friends and acquaintances, he has only two goals: to enjoy the pleasure of their company, and to make sure they enjoy his. He is not out to impress anyone.

Making Ready

Any time a gentleman plans to have guests in his home, he always . . .

. . . makes a quick list of things to do before his guests arrive and, if necessary, a list of the steps required to get dinner on the table. (Writing such things down is much more dependable, especially when both he and his guests are having fun.)

. . . makes sure his guests know where they may park, especially if he lives in a condominium or apartment complex.

. . . goes to the grocery store and the liquor store early in the day.

. . . makes sure there is plenty of ice.

. . . makes sure there are enough clean glasses, plastic or otherwise.

—

. . . checks the flatware and serving pieces he plans to use during the evening, and, if necessary, gives them a quick rub with a kitchen towel.

—

. . . determines what sort of music he wants to play.

—

. . . decides, more than a half hour before the guests arrive, what he will wear when he greets them.

—

. . . runs the garbage disposal, if he has one, and, at the very least, makes sure to empty the trash.

—

. . . puts out a fresh hand towel, or two.

—

. . . takes a shower, and puts on deodorant, a fresh pair of underwear, and a clean T-shirt.

—

. . . flushes and cleans the toilet.

. . . makes sure there is plenty of toilet paper.

. . . brushes the cat hair off the sofa—then confines the cat to a bedroom.

. . . hides or removes anything he is afraid could be broken.

If guests arrive uninvited, a gentleman does the best he can on short notice. So should the guests. In treating them kindly, the gentleman proves himself a saint, not merely a sanctuary.

101 Things Every Gentlemanly Host Should Know

When entertaining his friends or his coworkers, a gentleman does not spend more than he can comfortably afford. If he does so, he makes entertaining an extraordinary experience, when it should be a regular part of his life.

When entertaining guests, a gentleman never attempts a menu that is beyond his capabilities. If he must order takeout, he does so, without apologies.

If he can avoid it, a gentleman does not extend spur-of-the-moment invitations. Instead, he gives his guests plenty of time to plan their schedules and adjust them, if necessary, in order to take advantage of his hospitality.

A gentleman checks his china shelves and his linen closet before he invites guests into his home. The number of plates and napkins decrees the number of guests he can comfortably entertain.

If a gentleman can afford to buy more plates and napkins from time to time, he does so. Otherwise, he entertains fewer people, perhaps on a more frequent basis.

If a gentleman has announced that his party begins at 7 P.M., he is ready to greet his guests at 6:45. If any guest should arrive earlier than that hour, a gentleman feels perfectly free to suggest that the guest help out by slicing the limes.

If a gentleman must make the choice between using plastic and not entertaining, he uses plastic. Using plastic is far preferable to never entertaining at all. Someday, the china will come. If it never comes, at least there will have been parties.

Before a gentleman puts out his stainless (or his silverware, for that matter), he gives it a rub with a towel, just to make sure there are no dishwasher stains.

A gentleman owns at least one standard, all-purpose cookbook. He is not ashamed to ask his mother to give it to him for Christmas. Better yet, he is not ashamed to go to a bookstore and buy it for himself.

A gentleman never lets a guest stand alone in a corner. If he has planned the mix of his guests correctly, he can always spark up a conversation. He would never invite anyone into his home and allow that person to depart feeling that he or she has been ignored.

A gentleman allows his friends to enjoy themselves. However, he knows when to say, "Jim, wouldn't you like some soda now?" If Jim insists on having more vodka, a gentleman knows when to take his car keys, or when to call a cab.

When a gentleman is ready for the evening to end, he closes the bar. If there is no bar, he simply announces, "This has been a lot of fun, hasn't it? Wish I didn't have to get up at 7 A.M. tomorrow."

As a general rule, a gentleman does not play matchmaker. If he is particularly intuitive, he may feel free to invite a mix of single friends and then let nature take its course. He may, however, end up with a tedious evening for himself. Or he may end up with a slew of godchildren, each of whom will require presents on birthdays and holidays.

A gentleman knows how to introduce a friend to strangers and vice-versa.

A gentleman does not give surprise parties unless he is absolutely certain the honoree likes to be surprised.

In planning a party with a guest of honor, such as a birthday celebration or a bachelor party, he tries not to go too far in poking fun at the honoree.

A gentleman never hires a stripper.

If a guest arrives with a bottle of wine, unsolicited, a gentleman considers it a thank-you gift and feels no obligation to serve it. He simply accepts it and says, "You're very thoughtful. I'll be looking forward to enjoying this."

If a guest arrives with a casserole or an hors d'oeuvre, a gentleman finds some way to work it into the evening. Otherwise, he will be left with unexpected leftovers and a confused and insulted dinner guest.

A gentleman feels no necessity to write thank-you notes for gifts presented to him at his own party. If he should happen to receive thank-you notes for his hospitality, he considers himself extraordinarily blessed.

If a gentleman is serving iced tea or coffee, he makes sure to offer cream, sugar, and calorie-free sweeteners.

A gentleman makes sure that he has plenty of kitchen towels, or paper towels, available at any moment. Spills may, and invariably will, occur.

A gentleman always remembers that some of his guests may be non-drinkers, either for the evening or for life. He makes sure to put out some fruit juice, as well as some lime to go along with it.

A gentleman knows how to say, "Thank you. I hope you can come back again," when the evening is done. If guests linger too long, he knows how to say, "Now let me see, where did we put your coat?"

If a gentleman does not want his guests to smoke, he does not put out ashtrays.

If a gentleman has guests whom he knows to be smokers, he makes sure there is a place, perhaps on a balcony, perhaps in a garden, where they can smoke. In any case, he provides a receptacle in which they can extinguish their cigarette butts.

A gentleman always serves from the left and clears from the right.

If there are women at the table, a gentleman makes sure they are served first.

If there is a woman at the table, a gentleman, even if he is the host, does not lift his fork until she has lifted hers.

If a gentleman is serving dinner, he urges his guests to begin dining without him. Because he does not want them to be faced with cold soup or warm aspic, he means what he says.

If he owns enough flatware, a gentleman always makes sure new forks and knives are put out with every course. If he expects his guests to use the same fork for more than one course, he alerts them ahead of time.

When welcoming his friends—and especially when serving them food or drink—a gentleman makes sure his hands are washed and his fingernails are clean.

If a gentleman is expecting to host a particularly raucous evening, he makes sure to alert the neighbors.

If a party has gotten out of hand, a gentleman apologizes to his neighbors the next morning. On the night of the party, he will probably be in no condition to apologize appropriately, and his neighbors will be in no mood to appreciate the sincerity of his good intentions.

Whenever possible, a gentleman does not give parties that get out of hand.

A gentleman is always ready to offer his guests another drink, but he also makes sure dinner is on the table on time.

A gentleman knows how to open a bottle of wine.

If a gentleman is serving twist-top beers or sodas, he provides an obvious place for disposal of the caps.

A gentleman knows that by candlelight everyone looks more attractive—even family members, male or female.

A gentleman does not let spoiled or overripe food remain on his refrigerator shelves. He has no desire to serve ice that smells like two-week-old anchovy pizza.

If a gentleman wishes to have a blessing pronounced over his dinner, he makes sure to ask a person who is comfortable with pronouncing blessings. (He does not put a guest, even a minister, in an awkward position.) In any case, and unless a ranking clergyman is present, it is entirely appropriate for the host to pronounce the blessing himself.

On occasion, a gentleman scrubs his stove top, knowing full well that guests will see it and, if dismayed, question the safety of the food they will be eating.

A gentleman keeps a box of baking soda at the back of a shelf in his refrigerator.

A gentleman does not ask friends to help him clean the kitchen, unless, of course, he plans for them to linger long after the party is over.

If guests offer to help with the cleanup, and unless he is desperate for assistance, a gentleman says, "No, thank you. Let's have another cup of coffee (or another cognac). I'll think about the dishes another time."

When he entertains, either at home or in a restaurant, a gentleman makes sure to ask whether any of his guests have special dietary concerns. If some of his guests have medical conditions that restrict what they can eat, or if some of them are vegetarians—even vegans—he provides appetizing dishes they can enjoy.

A gentleman understands that some of his guests' religious convictions may determine what they may or may not eat. He hopes they will inform him of these restrictions so that he can offer a menu that all his guests can enjoy.

If a gentleman plans to entertain guests who must use a wheelchair, or who are otherwise physically challenged, he invites them to a location that is readily accessible to them. This may mean he cannot easily entertain them in his third-floor condo, but it does not mean he cannot invite them for drinks in a well-designed, up-to-date restaurant.

A gentleman knows how to make a martini, a Manhattan, and a Rob Roy.

A gentleman is capable of making a good pot of coffee on a few minutes' notice. The pot of coffee may be either regular or decaf. In either case, it is of the highest quality he can manage.

A gentleman knows that exotically flavored coffees are an acquired taste. Unless he is absolutely certain that everyone at his table enjoys them, he does not impose them upon his guests.

If a gentleman elects to serve flavored coffee, he makes sure unflavored coffee is available as well.

A gentleman never serves coffee until dessert.

When serving coffee, unless it is being offered to an unexpected overnight guest, a gentleman makes sure to provide milk or cream and sweeteners—both sugar and calorie-free substitutes.

Although some etiquette books demand that a gentleman never try out new recipes on his friends, a gentleman—at least at the beginning of his hosting career—seldom entertains anyone else. Therefore, he explains that he is experimenting and hopes that his friends will understand. At some later date he may try his friend-tested recipes on his boss, his priest, his rabbi, his minister, or his parents.

A gentleman never puts a wine bottle, white or red, directly on the table. A wine brick, for white wine, or a wine coaster, for red wine, is ideal, but a saucer under any bottle of wine will suffice.

A gentleman makes sure that white wine, whether a still wine like chardonnay or a sparkling wine like champagne, is well-chilled before he serves it. He lets it rest, for an hour if possible, in a bucket half filled with ice and a little water, before uncorking it.

A gentleman understands that red wines, fine or table quality, fare best when served at room temperature. However, he knows that the traditionally accepted definition of "room temperature" has nothing to do with overheated apartment buildings. If necessary, he lets a bottle of red wine rest in the refrigerator for a half hour or so before serving it.

A gentleman always opens the red wine, vintage or jug quality, ahead of time so that it can "breathe."

A gentleman never serves warm white wine, warm coffee, warm tea, or warm beer.

A gentleman knows that, even at a Super Bowl party, a few women add variety to an evening. They are also likely to help make sure the food gets served on time.

A gentleman may readily ask his mother to share her recipes. Except in moments of extreme desperation, he does not ask her to cook the meal.

A gentleman feels comfortable allowing guests into his kitchen, but he makes sure that all unsightly preparation has been finished and cleared away before they arrive.

A gentleman takes pains to plan the music for any evening. Only late in the night is it appropriate for him to ask, "Now, what would you folks like to hear?"

A gentleman always rinses and dries his salad greens before serving them. Otherwise his carefully prepared salad dressing will simply slide off the leaves. He knows that he can dry his greens with paper towels, but he also knows that salad spinners are modestly priced and available at any number of cook's shops and department stores.

When offering dinner to his friends—or even new acquaintances—at his own table, a gentleman may put their entrées before them, already on dinner plates, or he may allow them to serve themselves family-style. In either case, he waits until all his guests have been served before serving himself.

A gentleman may expect his guests to serve themselves, but he does not ask them to handle or pass hot serving dishes.

A gentleman limits the choice of dressings. He selects an appropriate dressing to complement the salad he has prepared.

When a gentleman is planning a cocktail party or a reception, he does not fret about whether there will be enough chairs. In fact, he hopes that a number of his guests will be forced to stand in order to encourage mingling.

When he is seating a large party of people, or when his dinner party involves people who are not well acquainted with one another, a gentleman may feel the need to use place cards (both to mix up the group cleverly and to help with the remembering of names). Otherwise, he simply tells his guests where he would like them to sit.

Even when the party consists entirely of good friends, a gentleman always "seats" his table carefully. He never seats husbands and wives, or dates, or couples next to one another. He assumes these persons will have plenty of time long after they have left his party to get on with their private lives.

When expecting guests in his home, a gentleman always leaves a candle—one that cannot easily be tipped over—burning in the bathroom. After his friends have gone home for the evening, a gentleman makes sure to blow out all the candles.

A gentleman never attempts to force a guest to clean his or her plate. Should a guest choose to eat nothing at all, a gentleman does not make a scene. He may with good reason, however, choose not to invite that guest to his dinner table again.

When arguments threaten to arise at the dinner table, a gentleman feels perfectly comfortable in saying, "I think we should change the subject."

When disputes arise during the cocktail hour or after dinner, over coffee or liqueurs, a gentleman does not attempt to squelch the debate. He does, however, attempt to prevent fistfights. If worse comes to worse, he may close the bar and announce that it is time for everyone to go home.

When a gentleman realizes that the dinner he has served is inedible, he admits it. Rather than let his guests go hungry, he has a pizza delivered and sends somebody out for ice cream.

Well before he begins serving dinner, a gentleman makes sure the dog, no matter how well behaved, is locked in a bedroom.

When a gentleman writes "RSVP" on an invitation, he expects a response from everyone he has invited, whether or not they plan to attend his gathering. He feels perfectly comfortable in attaching a deadline to his request for responses.

If a gentleman's dinner party is swiftly approaching and he has had no response from some of his invited guests, he gives them a buzz so that he can know whether or not to set a place for them.

If a gentleman's invitation is marked "Regrets only," he expects to hear only from those people on the guest list who will not be able to attend.

Unless he anticipates having to deal with an emergency, a gentleman does not answer the phone while entertaining guests in his home—particularly if he is entertaining only one guest. The advent of the answering machine allows him to check any incoming messages at a discreet moment and return them if necessity requires.

Unless an emergency looms, a gentleman does not carry his cell phone into a restaurant when he is hosting a dinner party. If there is a reason he may need to be contacted during the evening, he leaves the telephone number of the restaurant with anyone who may have a legitimate reason to give him a call.

If a gentleman must carry his cell phone into a restaurant, he turns the ringer setting to "vibrate." Before answering a call, he asks to be excused and leaves the table so he may conduct his conversation in private and so he does not inconvenience his guests.

A gentleman checks his smoke alarm on a regular basis, both for his own safety and for the safety of friends he may invite into his home.

A gentleman always has an extra umbrella for his guests to use.

A gentleman knows how to perform the Heimlich maneuver.

When a gentlman's invited guests arrive at his door, he never greets them in bare feet.

If a gentleman has lighted his dining table—or his bedside table—with candles, he makes sure they are safely extinguished when the evening is done.

Unless he has invited his guests into his home for the expressed purpose of watching television—for a sports event, say, or a rented movie—a gentleman leaves the television off when guests are present.

A gentleman does not host BYOB parties. He may suggest that guests bring a bottle of wine or a six-pack of beer—any beverage that may be consumed in its entirety during the evening—but he knows that he only creates confusion, and asks for trouble, by asking his guests to keep track of which liquor bottle belongs to whom. He also knows that at a BYOB party he will have almost no control over how much alcohol his guests consume.

Because he has planned his menu carefully, a gentleman does not clutter his dinner table with condiments. If a guest requests a certain sauce or flavoring, the gentleman does his best to satisfy his guest.

When planning to entertain guests in a restaurant, a gentleman always makes a reservation. If possible, he and his party show up precisely on time to claim their table. If they are running late for any reason, he phones ahead, knowing full well that in a busy, popular restaurant his table probably will not be held for more than a quarter hour.

When planning to entertain guests in a restaurant, a gentleman selects an establishment that is within his means financially.

Before entertaining guests in a restaurant, a gentleman makes sure he has the required amount of cash—or a valid credit card—with which to pay the bill.

A gentleman tips generously, but not lavishly or ostentatiously.

If a gentleman cannot find time to clean his house, he finds somebody to do it for him—even if he has to pay. In no case does he invite people into a filthy house and then expect them to consume food and drink.

When a gentleman serves takeout, he serves it on his own plates.

If a gentleman is fortunate enough to own sterling silver or silver plate, he never puts it in the dishwasher along with his stainless.

A gentleman owns a stock of white cotton cocktail napkins, although he may use paper ones from time to time—even with the most demanding of his friends.

If a gentleman invites his demanding friends into his home, he does not worry about living up to their overly meticulous standards.

A gentleman has as few demanding friends as possible.

A Gentleman Entertains

Anybody, Anywhere, Anytime

When a gentleman entertains, he may desire to go to a bit of trouble, exerting more than a little extra effort. The key is always thinking ahead, knowing where the mines are buried, then proceeding step by step. If he has done his job well, however, the effort will not show. His guests will enjoy themselves, and—at least as far as they know—so will he.

Having a Few Friends Over for Drinks

The Casual Cocktail Party

There are plenty of good reasons to get a group of friends together for drinks. The excuse can be a real occasion—a friend or coworker is relocating, a new friend has moved into town, it's the day before a holiday and nobody has to get up for work the next morning, or it's somebody's birthday—but a gentleman's best excuse for entertaining his friends is that he wants to enjoy their company. Maybe he hasn't seen them in awhile, at least not in a casual setting, or maybe he just needs to repay a few invitations. In any case, nothing works better than an easygoing Friday afternoon gathering for a half-dozen—or even a dozen—people of amiable temperament.

The Game Plan

1. If your space is limited, invite only as many friends as you can comfortably entertain. (If you can't invite everybody this time, there'll always be another Friday afternoon.)

2. When you extend your invitations by phone, by post, or by e-mail, make sure your guests understand that this is a casual gathering, not a sit-down supper. On the phone, for instance, it's easy to say, "I'm just having a few friends over for drinks." (That also lets your guests know they're not free to bring along an entourage.) On paper, you may want to be more specific. If you're planning to offer only beer and wine, let your guests know in your invitation what to expect.

3. Although you're only expecting your guests to hang around for a couple of hours, if you're giving them alcohol, you also have to give them food. This is especially true at the end of the workday when it's been hours since lunch and since some people may be stopping

by on the way home from the gym. If you've scheduled your party for a later hour, after a ball game or after the theater for example, a few light snacks will suffice.

4. When planning your hors d'oeuvre, have plenty of protein to help offset the alcohol, but offer some vegetables, too. You may have guests who are vegetarians, and some of your guests may not want to spoil their appetites for dinner. Sweet treats, such as cookies and mini-tarts, may be appropriate for a late-evening party; they will probably go untouched before 7 P.M.

5. At this type of party, you'll probably want to let your guests serve themselves. A bartender is unnecessary, and you won't want to be hovering over them. Therefore, you'll want to make sure the bar, however simple, is easily accessible and there are plenty of glasses. Your most vital role is keeping watch over the ice bucket. **You can never have too much ice.**

6. Even if you don't think any of your friends are teetotalers, you still must offer nonalcoholic

mixers, sodas, or juices for any nondrinkers in the group. You never know what has happened since the last time you saw them. Someone may have started a new medication.

7. If you're throwing a cocktail party at the end of a workday, make sure to leave the office in plenty of time so that you can have the bar set out and the music lined up before your guests arrive.

8. When you want your guests to start leaving, shut down the bar. (It may seem inhospitable, but it works.)

How to Make It Happen

1. Well ahead of time, think about what kind of food you want to serve. Make sure everything you offer is something you can pick up at the deli or something you can prepare ahead of time. (This is a small group; you want to be with your friends, not in the kitchen.) Remember, too, that this is a stand-up party. Plan to offer finger food that doesn't require plates. Shy away from dribbly sauces.

2. If you're planning to serve food that needs to be kept warm, you'll need a chafing dish. If you're serving food that needs to be kept cold, you'll need a bowl of ice.

3. Set up the bar well ahead of time. (*See How to Set Up a Bar on pages 42–43*)

4. If you've got enough glassware and cloth napkins to serve everybody, use them. Otherwise, use plastic and paper only. None of your friends should feel they aren't "good enough to use the real stuff."

5. If you're worried about the possibility that your friends may destroy the family china, don't use it.

6. If space allows, set up the bar and the food table in different parts of the room so the guests will be encouraged to mix and mingle. It's also a fact of life in the party-planning world that people tend to migrate away from the source of the music, whether it's a live band or a CD player. Thus, if you don't want them clustering around the bar, set it up relatively close to the sound system.

7. If you don't have room for a separate bar in your living room, use the kitchen counter. At intimate gatherings, people tend to hang out in the kitchen anyway.

8. If you're serving the hors d'oeuvres from your dining room table, remember to remove the chairs so that your guests don't have to reach over them.

9. At this sort of party, nobody really expects flowers. What's more, they take up space on the buffet. If you want to put out a few cut flowers in a vase—in a place where it won't easily be tipped over—you'll be doing all that's expected—and more.

Words to the Wise

At any party where alcohol is served, and particularly when guests are serving themselves, the host is well advised to keep an eye out for a friend who may have had too many. It is the host's responsibility—both legally and in terms of

good manners—to make sure the intoxicated guest does not get behind the wheel of any motorized vehicle. He finds some way for the overindulged guest to get home, either by arranging for a ride with a sober guest or by calling a cab.

A good host wants the memories of his party to be pleasant ones. While food and drink are important, he knows his hospitality and the spirit of the room are what people will recall in years to come.

How to Set Up a Bar

A good host offers a choice of Scotch, vodka, gin, white wine, beer, and, in the South, bourbon. He serves the wine in an ice bucket and keeps the beer cold, either in a cooler or in the refrigerator.

He makes sure to have plenty of ice, as well as a variety of mixers, not just for his drinking friends but for the pleasure of his nondrinking friends as well. His bar is never complete without freshly sliced lemons and limes, a

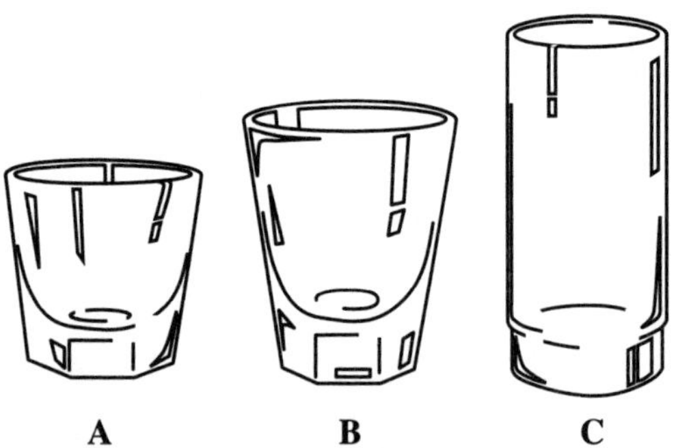

A. Old-fashioned
B. Double Old-fashioned
C. Highball

jigger, stirrers, plenty of glasses, a bottle opener, a corkscrew, and a stack of cocktail napkins.

For a party of ten to twelve guests, a well-stocked bar should include the following:

- 1 liter Scotch
- 1 liter vodka
- 1 fifth gin
- 1 fifth bourbon
- 4 liters tonic
- 4 liters club soda
- 1 small bottle dry vermouth
- 3 bottles white wine
- 3 six-packs beer
- A couple of fruit juices

For a party of this size, a host will want to have fifty pounds of ice, especially in the summer.

D. White Wine
E. Red Wine
F. Sturdy Plastic Tumbler (appropriate for everything)

Some Pickup Food You Can Do

At an early evening cocktail party, guests will probably be happy with a nice cheese tray, some chips and salsa, sliced fruit, and a couple bowls of mixed nuts. But here are a few easy treats to try if you want to go to just a little more trouble. (Because they're relatively hearty, any of these recipes would fit in nicely with a cocktail supper buffet.)

Shrimp with Guacamole on Tortilla Chips

Yield: 30–35 hors d'oeuvres

1 Tbs ground cumin

1 tsp salt

1 tsp garlic powder

1½ tsp chili powder

⅓ tsp cayenne pepper

¼ tsp black pepper

1 bag tortilla chips

1 cup guacamole

1 lb medium shrimp, cooked (31–35 count)

Mix dry ingredients together and sprinkle on shrimp. Broil for about three minutes. Spread guacamole on chips. Top with shrimp and serve.

Red-skin Potatoes with Cheese

Yield: 12 small servings

12 small red potatoes

½ cup mayonnaise

1 cup grated cheese (cheddar, Parmesan, Asiago—alone or in any combination)

Salt and pepper, to taste

Split potatoes in half lengthwise, and trim bottom so they sit flat. With a melon baller or a spoon, hollow out the middle of the potatoes. Cook hollow potatoes in boiling salted water until just tender (6–8 minutes). Remove and cool.

Preheat oven to 450°. Combine

mayonnaise and cheese in a medium bowl. Season with salt and pepper to taste. Spoon mixture into blanched potatoes to just fill the hole. Bake in oven until cheese mixture becomes golden brown (10 to 15 minutes). Remove and serve.

Note: The potatoes should be served warm. You may want to leave a few in the oven, if you don't have a chafing dish.

About Invitations

A good host attempts to give his guests plenty of notice. When he waits until the last minute to pull together a party, he must accept the fact that his friends may already have other plans.

Two weeks lead time is appropriate for a dinner party. One week is sufficient for a more casual gathering.

Whether he offers his invitation in writing or by phone, he makes sure to answer all the questions his guests might logically have. For written invitations, a gentleman makes sure to include the nature of the party (cocktails, supper, brunch, a birthday party for Mary Jane, or whatever), the

date, the hour, the address, specifics about what to wear, and the information his guests need in order to reply. If his guests will need instructions about parking, he includes those as well.

If a host needs an accurate headcount, he requests a reply by writing either "RSVP" or, more directly, "Please reply" at the bottom of his invitation, making sure to include his phone number. If his prospective guests have not responded by a reasonable time (forty-eight hours before the party), he may gracefully ask whether or not they plan to attend.

Invitations need not be elaborate. They may be handwritten, but, for larger parties, it is convenient to have them printed in quantity. Fill-in-the-blank invitations, adaptable to almost any occasion, are available at most stationery and card shops.

MiniBurgers

Yield: 8 mini burgers

1 lb ground chuck or ground round or ground sirloin

3 Tbs heavy cream

½ tsp Tabasco sauce

½ tsp salt

½ tsp pepper

Mini buns or small dinner rolls

8 dill pickle slices

Onion slices, optional

Cheese slices, optional

Mix beef, cream, Tabasco, salt and pepper in a medium bowl. Form eight small patties from this mixture. Either broil or fry the burgers to desired doneness, and place them on buns. Top with pickle, onion, and cheese if desired.

Note: These should be served warm.

ALONE AT LAST

A ROMANTIC DINNER FOR TWO

When a gentleman cooks and serves a romantic dinner, it is an intimate experience; it can also be nerve-wracking. The challenge, more than with any other type of entertaining, is to keep things simple so that the evening flows smoothly. Yes, you're trying to impress a person in whom you have a special interest, but you're also trying to have some time to breathe deeply and enjoy that person's company. It may just be supper, but it could be the most important evening of your life.

The Game Plan

1. Plan a menu you can handle, preferably one you can prepare almost entirely ahead of time. There will only be the two of you at this party; you don't want to seem neglectful by spending time in the kitchen whipping egg whites.

2. Find out ahead of time what your dinner guest likes to eat and drink. If the guest of honor has special dietary needs, respect them. (Lobster can be romantic, but not if it sends somebody to the emergency room.) If your guest prefers a particular wine or liquor, try to have it on hand.

3. This is no time to experiment with new dishes. If you must, do a practice dinner, trying it out on a trusting, understanding friend. You don't want to destroy a romantic mood by serving an overcooked chicken breast and some dried-up green peas. An inedible entrée can spoil everything.

4. Make sure you have all the necessary dishes, glassware, and linens—and make sure they are clean. It is perfectly acceptable to borrow a few pieces from friends or family; in fact, you may score points by letting it be known you've made that special effort.

5. Feel free to supplement your own cooking with takeout from a restaurant or catering service.

When it comes to dessert, a good bakery is invaluable. At that time in the evening, you should be able to relax and uncork the perfectly chilled champagne. If all has gone well, your guest won't care where you got the créme brûlée.

6. This may be the occasion that justifies springing for a bottle of especially good wine. If you are not an experienced oenophile, ask for advice at the liquor store. Over dinner, you can tell the story of how you made the purchase. Whether the subject is wine or the bond market, however, a gentleman never claims expertise that is not rightfully his.

How to Make It Happen

1. On this sort of occasion, a gentleman must be scrupulously organized and fully prepared, well before the doorbell rings. If any cooking remains to be done, it should require only minimal attention, perhaps a little basting, an occasional stirring, or a bit of warming up.

The salads should be waiting in the

refrigerator, not on the table. (A gentleman never appears to want to rush things.) If white wine is to be served, it is already on ice. If red wine is being served, it is already open.

2. Offer your guest a drink, pour yourself one, and then sit down and talk. By doing so, you will establish a reputation as a self-confident, attentive, sublimely organized sort of guy. A gentleman is well advised, on potentially romantic evenings, not to linger too long over cocktails.

3. On this evening, it is the host's job to be the server. He lights the candles, pours the wine, brings the food to the table, and clears away the empty plates. He may allow his guest to help out by filling the water glasses. Otherwise, the host handles every detail.

4. You may either prepare the plates in the kitchen, or the two of you may serve yourselves—and each other—at the table.

5. When you return the dirty plates to the kitchen, give them a quick rinse in the sink and slip them in the dishwasher, if you have one.

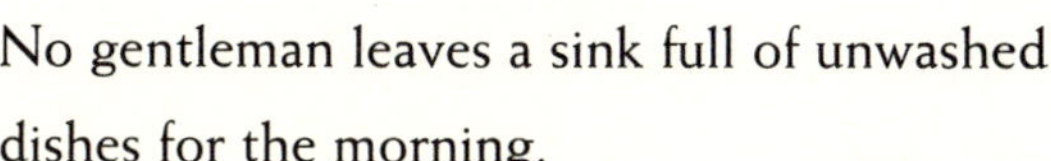

No gentleman leaves a sink full of unwashed dishes for the morning.

Words to the Wise

When it's just the two of you, attentiveness is everything. Of course, you want a romantic dinner to be elegant, but elegance has nothing to do with ostentatiousness. Keep it simple, keep the music soft, and keep your company entertained.

Love Me, Love My Vinaigrette

Here's a suggested menu that's perfect for two. It's relatively simple to prepare. It can be done ahead of time. It includes a number of basic dishes that any gentleman should have in his repertoire. And best of all, it should lie lightly on the stomach. There is garlic involved, so make sure both of you eat some of everything.

Crippen Salad and Vinaigrette Dressing

Yield: 4 servings

Dressing

4 Tbs olive oil

1 Tbs vinegar

¼ tsp salt

½ tsp dry mustard

½ tsp fresh ground pepper

Salad

1 to 2 large bunches watercress,
or other mixed greens, cleaned and stemmed

1 can (15 oz) hearts of palm, sliced

1 cup sliced fresh mushrooms

⅓ cup sliced almonds, toasted

Combine all the dressing ingredients in a jar and shake vigorously. Just before serving, toss all salad ingredients and place on chilled plates. Pour the dressing over the salad and serve.

Kentucky Bourbon Pork Tenderloin

Yield: 4–6 servings

1 pork tenderloin (2½ to 3 pounds)

¼ cup soy sauce

¼ cup bourbon

2 Tbs brown sugar

¼ cup melted butter

Garlic salt and pepper, to taste

Place the tenderloin in a glass casserole dish. In a small bowl, combine the soy sauce, bourbon, and brown sugar. Pour the sauce over the pork and refrigerate for several hours.

Return meat to room temperature. Preheat oven to 350°. Place marinated tenderloin on a wire rack on a cookie sheet. Drizzle with melted butter and sprinkle with garlic salt and pepper. Bake for 45 minutes, basting frequently.

Wild Rice

Yield: 4 servings

2½ cups water

1 cup wild rice

¼ tsp salt

1 tsp butter

Place ingredients in a saucepan. Bring to a boil. Reduce heat and simmer for 40 to 45 minutes or until rice is tender, stirring occasionally.

Roasted Roma Tomatoes

Yield: 6 servings

6 Roma tomatoes

Garlic salt and pepper, to taste

¼ cup olive oil

1 tsp fresh herbs (basil, oregano, marjoram . . .)

1 tsp Parmesan cheese

Preheat oven to 350°. Slice tomatoes lengthwise. Sprinkle with garlic salt and pepper. Drizzle with oil and bake for 45 minutes. Sprinkle with fresh herbs and cheese in the final five minutes of baking.

For dessert, have something chocolaty from a good bakery. Or go out for a scoop of good ice cream or a piece of pie.

About Flowers and Candles

A romantic dinner table really needs fresh flowers and the soft glow of candles. But the flowers need to be an asset to the table, not an obstruction. Arrange them in a low vase or bowl, so they don't prevent your making eye contact with your guest. Shy away from overly aromatic blooms such as heavy-scented lilies, which can overpower even the strongest passion.

Candlelight makes anybody look more attractive, including the gentleman himself. As with flowers, candles should be positioned so that they are not an obstacle or a safety hazard. The host lights them just before serving the salad course, and he makes sure to snuff them out before leaving the table. (When snuffing out candles, he cups one hand behind the flame, to prevent hot wax spattering across the table and onto his guest.)

In order to make sure that his candles can be easily lighted, a clever host tests them ahead of time, letting them burn for a few minutes so that some of the wax slides away from the wick.

Relative Success

Holidays with the Family

During holidays such as Mother's Day and Father's Day, Thanksgiving, and Christmas, and celebrations such as birthdays and anniversaries, many families enjoy getting together. Often these get-togethers are elaborate, daylong affairs, staged at the ancestral home (or the parents' condo). On such occasions, however, you do not have to be just another victim of congealed salad and rock-hard fruitcake. One of these holidays, you may even feel the urge to take charge and host the family yourself.

The Game Plan

1. Although you're hosting the celebration, you'll still want to let your mother think she's in charge. Get her to agree to the deal before you broach the idea with anyone else. Ask her to help you plan the menu, so you don't forget

who's traditionally responsible for which special dish, but make the calls yourself.

There is one exception to this rule: Don't ask your mother to plan the Mother's Day lunch.

2. Make it clear what menu item, or items, you plan to provide. Do not let your mother bring everything.

3. If it's appropriate in your family, plan some sort of group activity after the meal. On Thanksgiving Day or New Year's Day, there's always a football game on television. On Christmas Day, everybody can go to a movie. On the Fourth of July, you can go to the park and watch fireworks.

4. Set clear parameters as to when you want the guests (they're family, but they're still guests) to arrive and when you expect the gathering to break up. By setting a clear time frame, you may prevent Aunt Mildred from arriving at noon with a casserole that needs to heat up for half an hour, forcing everybody else (and the turkey) to cool their heels.

5. Because it's your house, you can invite a few of your own friends if you want. Just make sure there's room for everybody to sit down.

How to Make It Happen

1. Start making your calls in plenty of time, determining what each family member will provide. Sketch out a skeleton menu and ask family members to help you fill in the blanks. You may know, well ahead of time, what Aunt Mildred is going to bring, but at least you'll end up with some semblance of a balanced menu. You may even avoid too many duplicate mushroom soup casseroles.

Under no circumstances may you say, "Don't worry. We've got everything covered; don't bring a thing."

2. If you do not own enough dishes, flatware, glasses, and serving pieces for an event of this magnitude, borrow them from family members. Pick them up ahead of time, but you'll prevent

confusion if you let the lenders take them home after the celebration is done.

3. Decide how the meal will be served. If there is not enough room around your dining room table, let them serve themselves buffet style (*see glossary on page 175*). If you don't have a dining room table, use the kitchen counter. Even if everyone can fit around the table, let them serve themselves, family style (*see glossary on page 175*).

4. By all means, if your father always carves the turkey at his house, let him carve the turkey at your house, too.

5. Even if you cannot seat everyone at one table, make sure there are plenty of flat surfaces on which guests can rest their plates. Set up a card table, clear off the coffee table, stack up some books. Do whatever it takes to prevent spills and broken glassware.

6. If there are small children in your family, do the best you can to kid-proof your home. Although their parents should be keeping watch (they *are* guests in your home, after all), it's still

your responsibility to put away the breakables. You might even want to invest in, or borrow, toddler-proof outlet caps.

7. If you volunteer to provide the main course, such as the turkey or ham, you do not have to cook it yourself. Order it instead from a grocery store, restaurant, or gourmet store. Make the reservation in plenty of time, telling the staff at the store or restaurant exactly how many people will be present. If they're a reputable establishment, they'll tell you exactly how big a ham or turkey you need.

8. Holidays allow for an exception to one of the cardinal rules of entertaining. On these occasions the host may ask anyone to help set the table and set out the food. These are also the only days on which he may let his guests pitch in if they offer to help with the cleanup.

Words to the Wise

Family gatherings are times of traditional celebration, but they are often times for traditional squabbling as well. In the bosom of the family, some blood relations may treat each other more rudely than they would a total stranger. As the host of a gathering, a gentleman does his best to short-circuit such ugliness. He may even go so far as to say, "This is my house, and I suggest we not get into that argument today." If he is lucky, his guests, finding themselves on alien turf, may be on their better-than-usual behavior.

Recipes Even a Mother Could Love

Even if you don't provide the main course, you can still amaze the elders with a spectacular hot dish or dessert, every bit as rich as anything your grandmother could make. Go ahead, it's Thanksgiving. Have some cholesterol.

Dauphinoise Potatoes

Yield: 5–6 servings

5 or 6 potatoes

Salt and pepper, to taste

1 cup shredded cheddar cheese

4 Tbs butter, softened

¾ cup Parmesan cheese, grated

Heavy cream

Preheat oven to 350°. Peel and thinly slice the potatoes. Do not wash slices. Lay half of the slices in a glass casserole dish. Salt and pepper these slices to taste. Cover with the cheddar cheese. Add remaining slices of potatoes. Dot these with the soft butter and sprinkle with the Parmesan cheese. Add heavy cream to come halfway up the dish. Bake in the oven for one hour.

Bread Pudding

Yield: 8–10 servings

12 slices day old bread
4 whole eggs
1 cup sugar
1 tsp vanilla extract
4 egg yolks
⅛ tsp salt
4 cups milk
1 cup heavy cream
Confectioners' (powdered) sugar

Remove the crusts from the bread. Cut into bite-sized cubes. Place the cubes in a glass casserole dish. In a medium bowl, beat together the eggs, egg yolks, sugar, salt, milk, and vanilla.

Preheat oven to 375°. Over medium-low heat, warm the cream in a saucepan. Once warm, add the cream to the egg mixture. Pour over bread pieces. Bake in the oven for 45 minutes. Dust finished pudding with confectioners' sugar.

Menu Checklist for Family Gathering

APPETIZER/HORS D'OEUVRE

What Kind?________________________

Who's Bringing It?_____________________

SALAD (may be more than one)

What Kind?________________________

Who's Bringing It?_____________________

ENTRÉE

What Kind?________________________

Who's Bringing It?_____________________

VEGETABLES (including casseroles)

What Kind?________________________

Who's Bringing It?_____________________

CONDIMENTS (pickles, olives, etc.)

What Kind?________________________

Who's Bringing It?_____________________

DESSERTS

What Kind?________________________

Who's Bringing It?_____________________

BREAD

What Kind?________________________

Who's Bringing It?_____________________

BEVERAGES

What Kind?________________________

Who's Bringing It?_____________________

AMONG FRIENDS

THE DINNER PARTY (4 – 8 GUESTS)

A small dinner party is one of life's great communal experiences. A few friends come together for good food and good conversation, and the host has a chance to try out a few recipes, perhaps say thank-you for some past hospitality, and enjoy the company of people whom he values. Such gatherings offer the perfect opportunity to introduce new acquaintances, or out-of-town visitors, to your circle of friends. By inviting his friends to such a party a gentleman pays them the greatest compliment possible.

The Game Plan

1. A good host remembers that, although he may like all his friends, they may not like one another. He plans his guest list accordingly. He will be wise to invite a mix of good talkers and good listeners, remembering, however, that one

boorish extrovert can ruin the evening for a self-conscious newcomer.

2. A gentleman does not need a special occasion to host a dinner party. However, such parties are a splendid means of celebrating a birthday, a promotion, or some other happy transition. If such an occasion is being celebrated, the host makes sure all the guests are apprised of it ahead of time. If gifts are not to be brought, he makes sure everyone is informed of that decision as well.

3. Especially when entertaining a small group of friends, a host must be conscious of what his guests can and cannot eat. The vegetarian may become ill at the sight of a filet mignon, and an apparent omnivore may harbor an allergy to shellfish. If a gentleman is not familiar with his guests' dietary restrictions, he simply asks them, when extending his invitation: "Is there anything you do not eat?" It is then the guest's responsibility to tell the truth.

If the host is planning to serve dishes that are in the least bit unusual—spicy paella, for example—he lets his guests know ahead of time. (The paella may, in fact, be the excuse for the party, and a guest may have to decline if he or she cannot eat spicy foods.) The host hopes that his guests, being his friends, will let him know if their diets are in any way, or for any reason, restricted so that he can do his best to plan a menu everyone can enjoy.

4. A good host plans a menu that will not keep him confined to the kitchen throughout the cocktail hour. When he must be away from his guests, he may ask one of his friends to keep the glasses filled—and the conversation going.

5. In planning a dinner party, a host doesn't need to serve up a Sunday-dinner-style groaning board. Instead, a well-planned menu will keep everybody happy. It will also help keep the host out of the kitchen.

How to Make It Happen

1. Decide early on, before you invite even one guest, just how many people you can comfortably entertain. Be realistic about how much space you have, how much time you have, and how much money you have.

2. A telephone invitation is probably most appropriate for a small dinner party. Try to give your guests at least a week's notice. Two weeks is better still.

3. Once you know who is coming, decide where they will sit. If you plan to serve your guests buffet style, give some thought to where you will serve the food—on a table, on a sideboard, on a kitchen counter—and where they will put their plates while they will eat.

4. Set the table well ahead of time, perhaps even the night before the party. Nothing could be worse than discovering, at the last minute, that you do not have enough forks to go around.

5. Be dressed and ready well before your guests are scheduled to arrive.

6. Although you may plan to offer your guests cocktails, they will not expect a full bar. Just set out the basic liquors, some mixers, a few simple garnishes, and a well-filled ice bucket. As host, you may wish to fix a first drink for each guest, but after that they may be on their own, with the gentlemen in the group mixing drinks for the ladies.

In any event, fruit juice or sodas must be offered as a thoughtful gesture to your nondrinking guests. If wine is served at the dinner table proper, however, it may be assumed that nondrinkers will be happy with water, since the taste of fruit juices or sodas may not compliment the menu the host has prepared.

7. Even if he and his friends are not drinkers, the host should include a "cocktail hour" in the evening's agenda. He may offer spicy tomato juice or some other not-too-sweet libation, but he makes sure not to rush his guests directly from the door to the dinner table. Even if they are good friends, they will savor the opportunity

to chat. What's more, this gentle pause in the evening allows time for the arrival of any stragglers. It also gives the host one last chance to get himself organized.

8. If it is at all possible, a small dinner party—even if it is served from a buffet—should be served on real plates, and real glasses should be used. Everything must be clean and freshly polished. The cocktail napkins may be paper, but the dinner napkins should be cloth. If the host has a good tablecloth, he uses it on nights such as these.

9. No matter how simple his menu, a host is well advised to make a list of the steps that lie before him in getting dinner on, and off, the table.

10. In no case does the host of a small dinner party allow his guests to assist in preparing the meal (unless the party is a joint effort by a couple of friends who fancy themselves gourmet chefs). Nor does he permit them to assist in the cleanup. He may allow them to

assist in last-minute tasks such as filling the water glasses, lighting the candles, or bringing the appetizer tray to the kitchen after cocktails. Otherwise, their only job is to sit, be served, and make clever conversation.

11. His friends may have known one another for years, but the host still feels free to "seat" the table, making sure that couples are not seated together and that two nontalkers are not seated side by side. If there is a guest of honor at this sort of small gathering, the host seats him between two particularly convivial guests.

12. When serving dinner at the table, a gentleman serves from the left and clears from the right. He removes no more than two plates from the table at a time. He does not stack dirty plates on top of one another.

13. The host does not leave dirty dishes on the table between courses. Before serving after-dinner drinks, he clears everything away and brushes the crumbs from the table.

How to Set a Table

A gentleman knows how to set an elegant, if rudimentary, dinner table. The basic equipment is arranged in this manner:

WHEN SALAD IS SERVED AS A FIRST COURSE

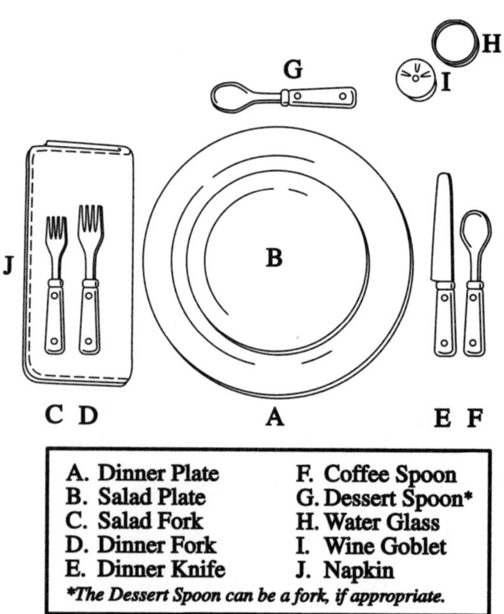

When Salad is Served

along with the Entrée

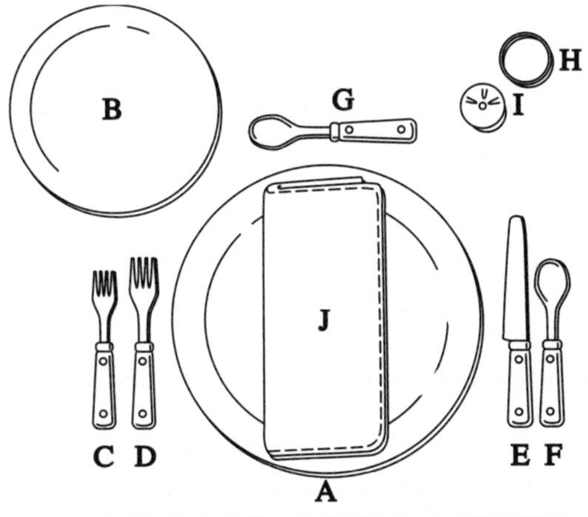

A. Dinner Plate
B. Salad Plate
C. Salad Fork
D. Dinner Fork
E. Dinner Knife
F. Coffee Spoon
G. Dessert Spoon*
H. Water Glass
I. Wine Goblet
J. Napkin

The Dessert Spoon can be a fork, if appropriate.

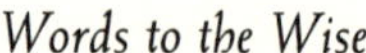

Words to the Wise

At a small dinner party, the conversation is as important as the food. At least while the party is at the table, a good host attempts to steer talk away from topics that are likely to spark an argument. After dinner, back in the living room, guests may debate as heartily, and as heatedly, as they like, provided they keep their tempers under control.

Nothing's Too Good for My Friends

At any party, especially a small one for people he likes, the host wants to spend as little time as possible among the pots and pans. Here's a quick, but classic, pasta sauce that can be adapted for meat eaters or vegetarians. Add a nice salad, a crisp green vegetable, a good loaf of bread, and one of the all-time favorite desserts, and you've got an evening well worth remembering.

Thirty-Minute Tomato Sauce With Fresh Herbs Over Pasta

(This sauce is hearty enough to make your vegetarian guests happy, but chicken may be added if you like.)

Yield: 6–8 servings

¼ cup extra virgin olive oil

1 medium-sized yellow onion, chopped

1 garlic clove, chopped

¼ cup chopped fresh parsley

1 can (28 oz) whole or diced tomatoes, juice included

Salt

1 pound pasta

1/4 cup chopped fresh basil

Parmesan cheese, grated

Heat the oil in a heavy saucepan over medium-low heat. (Don't let it get too hot.) Test the oil with a sliver of onion—it should sizzle. Add onion, garlic, and parsley and sauté until the onion and garlic are soft. (Do not let

them burn.) Add the tomatoes, with their liquid. (If using whole tomatoes, break them up with a wooden spoon.) Increase the heat to medium high to simmer rapidly. Stir frequently until the liquid evaporates (about 20 minutes).

Bring to a boil a large kettle of salted water (5 or 6 quarts). Add the pasta and cook according to package directions. A couple of minutes before the pasta is done, add the chopped basil to the pasta sauce.

Drain the pasta and divide it among the dinner plates. Top with the sauce and grated Parmesan cheese. Do not smother the pasta with the sauce, and go light on the cheese. Serve immediately.

Note: To make serving even easier, cook the pasta ahead of time until it is almost done. Drain it and set aside. Then, a few minutes before you're ready to serve it, finish cooking it in the tomato sauce.

Pecan Pie

Yield: 6–8 servings

3 eggs, slightly beaten

1 cup light corn syrup

1 cup sugar

2 Tbs butter or margarine, melted

1 tsp vanilla

1½ cups pecans

1 nine-inch frozen deep-dish unbaked pie crust

Preheat oven to 350°. Mix all the ingredients in a large bowl. Pour the mixture into the pie crust. Bake on the cookie sheet for 45 to 50 minutes or until golden brown.

How to Serve Dinner

When the host announces that dinner is ready, he invites his guests to the table and shows them to their places. He proceeds to serve the meal as follows:

- If he is serving a salad, the host places the salad plates directly on the dinner plates (which have already been set).
- When the guests have finished their salads, the host removes the salad plates. If he plans to serve the dinner plates in the kitchen, he takes them away at the same time. The salad forks are cleared away with the salad plates.
- The host either serves the dinner plates in the kitchen, or he brings the main course and its side dishes to the table, where the guests serve themselves.
- The host may wish to fill his guests' wine glasses for the first time himself. From then on, at an intimate gathering of friends, he encourages them to serve themselves, passing the bottle from person to person.

- When his guests have finished the main course, with second helpings if they are offered, the host clears away the dinner plates along with the dinner forks and knives.
- Salad may follow the entrée, if the host prefers.
- Finally, the host serves dessert. If he has not already placed the dessert forks or spoons on the table, he may bring them out along with the dessert itself. If there is coffee, he serves it now.

Private Screening

Gatherings around the Television

Whether it's the Super Bowl, the NCAA Basketball Championship, the Oscars, or even the Miss America Pageant, the tradition of inviting friends over to share a major television spectacle is as old as television itself. Invariably, these are niche-interest events since everybody is supposed to be there with one purpose, and only one purpose, in mind. Consider it a bonding experience. If you want to start cementing some friendships, start melting some cheese.

The Game Plan

1. In planning this kind of party, the host assumes that he knows a number of people who actually want to watch the television event in the company of others. Still, he carefully plans his guest list to include, for the

most part, people who really care about the event. If he invites one guest who isn't into the game, he makes sure to invite others of a like mind. Then he makes sure they have a place where they can enjoy themselves without disturbing the diehard fans in the living room.

2. If the host invites ardent fans of both teams, he makes sure to include a fair representation from both sides. Nobody likes to be shouted down when he gets excited about his team's seventy-five-yard run.

3. The host recognizes that the point of the party is to watch television. He does not invite more guests than can comfortably gather around his television set.

4. Food is not the real point of this party. This is a perfect time to pick up subs or have a pizza delivered. Neither is fine china and glistening stemware required. Bring out the plastic plates and glasses. They won't break when somebody slings them across the room.

5. More than some other types of parties, this kind of bash can get boisterous. If you live in a condo or apartment complex, let the neighbors know ahead of time that you're planning a gathering that could get rowdy. Soothe their fears the best way you can, perhaps invite them to drop in for a beer.

6. Because all his guests will be glued to the television until the commercial breaks, the host knows that they are all likely to run for the bathroom at the same time. It is especially important on such occasions to have plenty of toilet paper—as well as a toilet that works.

How to Make It Happen

1. On the morning of the big event, clean the television screen and put out enough chairs and cushions to allow each of your guests a good view of the screen. Don't worry too much about comfort. They will logically expect that somebody will have to sit on the floor.

2. Make sure you know when the game, or the awards show, actually begins, and plan your party accordingly. It's a good idea to invite guests as much as an hour ahead of the starting time, so they can have a drink and begin to graze the buffet.

3. Make sure you know which channel will be carrying the game or show. If the show is being carried on cable, make sure your service includes the right channel.

4. Once you've set the food out on the buffet, it will probably stay there until the party is done. Keep that fact in mind when planning the menu. Steer away from gloppy dips that can congeal in a couple of hours. If you're serving anything that must be heated in a chafing dish, remember to stir it once in a while.

It's best not to require too much manual dexterity from your guests. Avoid serving anything that can't be eaten without a knife and fork. A spoon for baked beans is about as complex as you should get.

5. You may put out a full bar if you like, but beer and wine and sodas probably will fulfill the expectations of even your most demanding guests. If you're providing a keg, put it on a porch, on a balcony, or in the garage—someplace that's shady in the summer and cold in the winter months.

6. Provide plenty of napkins. Remember, people will be eating off their laps and sitting on the floor.

Words to the Wise

To rev up the excitement while the big game or the big awards show is going on, you can start a pool, encouraging guests to pick the winners or predict a point spread. That kind of activity helps keep the crowd interested in the event, even if it's a lackluster year. It also helps guarantee that they'll stay around until the end of the show. However, a pool can also rev up the air of competition in the room. Sporting events are supposed to be fun. You don't want your party to turn into the WWF.

Stuff Guys Will Eat

The point here is to keep it hearty and keep it simple. You can depend on the old staples such as chips and salsa and a tray of cheese cubes. (This is a great time to shop at one of those huge wholesale grocery stores. They usually have a great shrimp and cocktail sauce at a reasonable price.) You'll still want a couple of main attractions as part of your spread. Add some cornbread and crackers and some pick-up desserts. With all that, your guests won't have any doubts that they've had a full meal.

Chili

Yield: 6–8 servings

2 lb ground beef

1 tsp black pepper

1 green bell pepper, chopped

½ onion, chopped

1 tsp garlic salt

3 Tbs chili powder

1 can (16 oz) light red kidney beans or chili beans

1 can (16 oz) tomato sauce

Brown the ground beef in a skillet, breaking the meat into small pieces. Add garlic salt, black pepper, and chili powder. Add bell pepper and onion. Then, add the beans and tomato sauce. Cook for 30 minutes to an hour and serve.

Bachelor Soup

Yield: 6–8 servings

1 lb ground beef

1 can (16 oz) mixed vegetables

1 can (10 oz) Rotel tomatoes and green chilies

1 can (13 oz) Spanish rice

1 can (14½ oz) stewed tomatoes

1 can (17 oz) cream-style corn

Lightly brown ground beef in a kettle. Add the remaining ingredients and simmer for 40 minutes.

Good Keg Manners

A major bowl game seems to cry out for a keg of beer. Kegs come in all sorts of sizes—full size, medium size (pony), as well as even smaller sizes, which can be filled with more exotic beers and ales.

Kegs may usually be rented any place beer is sold in quantity. It should already be chilled and should come with a tap, which you push into the top of the keg, twist, and pump.

A gentleman always remembers to give the keg a few pumps after pouring his beer to build up the pressure for the next person in line.

FENDER BENDER

POTLUCK TAILGATE PARTY

There's nothing scarier than the prospect of a no-holds-barred potluck party: two dozen people show up for the pregame tailgater, everybody's brought potato salad, and nobody brought forks to eat it with. This sort of party lets everybody participate, but like any other team effort, it requires a coach who knows what he's doing. In this case, being a host doesn't mean you have to do everything. It does mean, however, that you have to make sure all the right things, and only the right things, happen.

The Game Plan

1. Whether it's a tailgate party before the homecoming game or a going-away party for the favorite secretary at the office, a potluck demands that somebody be in charge. If the host wants this party to work, he must select

the time and the place, and determine at least the outline of a workable, well-balanced menu. It's fun to let everybody pitch in, but in the end, you may decide it would have been easier to do it all yourself.

2. This sort of party is not the same thing as a holiday dinner where the host asks the participants what they would like to bring. This is no job for the fainthearted. As the organizing force, a gentleman is brave enough to tell each person what he or she is expected to bring. You will attempt to be flexible and well-mannered, of course, but you will also be the only one who actually knows how many people are already lined up to bring fried chicken. By simply suggesting, "Everybody bring your favorite dish," you're setting up a culinary minefield.

3. Create a checklist, like the one suggested for family holiday dinners (*see page 67*), and stick to it. If you're organizing an office potluck, you may simply want to post the list on a bulletin board and let people sign up to bring various

dishes. Still, the host must monitor the list daily, making sure all the gaps are filled.

4. When you're creating your checklist, remember to assign someone to bring the paperware and plastic cups. Invariably, there's somebody in every group who will be relieved to take this assignment, either because he can't cook or because he hates to. Your party may even include a few individuals who'd just like to pitch in a little cash to underwrite the keg or pay for the wine.

5. Don't forget to assign someone to bring the ice and the condiments.

6. It ought to go without saying, but we'll say it anyway: If the potluck party is given in honor of a friend or coworker, the honoree must not be asked to help throw the party.

How to Make It Happen

1. Well ahead of time, scope out the party site, whether it's a parking lot outside the stadium or the conference room in your office

suite. A little troubleshooting can prevent last-minute surprises.

2. When establishing the site of a tailgate party, it's not enough to say, "You'll see us. We'll be the ones in the white pickup truck in the parking lot." Be as specific as you can and arrive well ahead of time to stake out a spot where your friends can find you easily. It may help to attach a flag or pennant to your car antenna, but only if the pennant isn't exactly like hundreds of others in the parking lot.

3. When selecting the party site, make sure it is one where tailgating is permitted. If you plan to serve alcoholic beverages, make sure that's permitted too.

4. Even if the party is to be held in your own home, you'll need to give some thought as to where guests will set out their dishes. Remember, although potluck food should be ready to eat when it arrives, some guests will still want to do some last-minute preparation. Set aside some space for them, and make sure the oven is clean.

5. When organizing a tailgate party, or any other sort of potluck, make sure the participants know what time they are expected to arrive and what time the meal will be served. The goal is to have a good time, enjoy your meal, and have everything cleaned up and packed away well before kickoff—or, in the case of an office party, before it's time to go back to work.

6. If you're organizing an alfresco event, remind the guests that they may want to bring folding chairs, tables, or blankets. Otherwise, they'll have to be content to stand and eat from the hood of the car.

7. Once the party's over, organize a cleanup brigade, whether the site is a parking lot or the office break room. Leave the place cleaner than it was when you found it. A gentleman tailgater always packs a couple of trash bags.

Words to the Wise

A potluck party is a group effort. One of the goals is to make everyone feel included and

important. As host, although you've organized the entire event, you must also acknowledge everyone else's efforts. They may forget to say, "Thank you, Larry, for making this happen," but you must never forget to say, "Thank you, Sarah, for bringing the wonton roll-ups."

For General Audiences

You may not be able to please all the people all the time, but you can try. This dip, impressively rich and absolutely no trouble to make, includes something for almost everybody.

Multi-Layered Dip

Yield: 12 servings

1 carton (8 oz) sour cream

1 package (¼ oz) taco seasoning

1 can (16 oz) refried beans

1 carton (6 oz) avocado dip

1 can (4½ oz) chopped ripe olives

2 small tomatoes, diced

1½ cups Monterey Jack or cheddar cheese, shredded

1 bag tortilla chips

In a small bowl, mix the sour cream and taco seasoning. In a serving bowl, layer the beans, sour cream mix, avocado dip, olives, tomatoes, and cheese. Serve with tortilla chips.

Food to Go

Just because it's your favorite dish, it may not be right for a potluck party, particularly if that party is taking place outside, at the height of summer. If the party is an outdoor affair, discourage your potlucking friends from bringing anything that involves eggs (and that includes anything involving mayonnaise) and milk or cream.

Frozen dishes, or dishes that need to remain chilled should be thoroughly chilled, or even frozen, before leaving home. (Make sure to have ice on hand.) If a dish must be served piping hot, strike it from your list of outdoor potluck possibilities, unless you're willing to bring along a chafing dish and a can of Sterno.

If you plan to transport food very often, you might as well start collecting some plastic dishes with snap-on airtight lids. You may want to invest in a sturdy cooler and maybe even a heavy-duty picnic basket with good, strong handles and spaces for storing dishes and flatware as well as food.

Outside Chances

Weekend Cookouts

Ever since the Neanderthals started cooking mammoth steaks over a campfire, grilling has been a guy thing. Every man who's ever heated up charcoal thinks he knows everything there is to know about serving up a steak that's perfectly seared on the outside but pink and juicy inside. He may know his way around a marinade, but there's more to planning a cookout than putting a few T-bones on soak.

The Game Plan

1. If you're planning a cookout menu that offers only burgers or steaks, or even grilled chicken, make sure you're inviting only your meat-eating friends. Really appealing veggie burgers are available in almost every grocery store these days, so nobody needs to be left out of the cookout crowd. It's your job, as host, to think ahead.

2. A successful cookout is all about thorough preparation. It's imperative that the grill be freshly scrubbed before you turn on the gas or start heating the charcoal. (Do not assume that the flames will simply burn off any unappetizing gunk. You'll end up with chicken that tastes like last week's pork chops.) Organize your equipment—tongs, long-handled fork, water bottle, and platters—ahead of time and have them close at hand, ready to use at any instant.

3. Don't wait until the guests get there to find out that you don't have enough charcoal or starter. Don't risk the sad surprise of an empty propane tank. Check your supplies at least twenty-four hours out.

4. If you plan to have your guests arrive before you start heating the grill, make sure you provide them with the drinks and snacks necessary to keep them occupied while you attempt to achieve those perfect, gray-dusted briquettes.

5. As a general rule, a good host already has the coals started before his guests arrive.

6. If your grill is located in a backyard or on an open patio, it's a good idea to have an emergency plan of action in mind in case of rain. It's not the safest idea to move a flaming bed of coals into a garage or onto a balcony. If worse comes to worse, you may have to cook your sirloins under the broiler. They'll make a mess, but, faced with an act of God, there's not much else a gentleman can do.

7. Even on the breeziest evening, don't forget the bug spray. A few citronella candles on the table are a good idea, too.

How to Make It Happen

1. If your recipes call for marinating meat or vegetables, plan to get them in the sauce hours ahead of time.

2. A gentleman must have enough of everything to serve everybody. It simply won't do to offer steaks to a few and burgers to everyone else.

How to Start a Charcoal Grill

1. Stack the briquettes in a pyramid.
2. Pour lighter fluid over the stack of coals.
3. Carefully light with a match, making sure to stand clear of the top of the coals.
4. Charcoal is ready when 70 percent of it is ashed over (approximately 15–20 minutes).

3. It's all right to invite friends to chat with you while you monitor the grill, but don't let them distract you. In the cookout business, a few lost seconds can spell disaster.

4. Because grilled food needs to be served right away, all plates and utensils must be ready for immediate use. You may want to ask your guests to bring their plates to the grill so that you can serve them. This process also makes it easier for them to select a steak or burger that's cooked the way they prefer—rare, medium, or well-done.

5. Organizing the cooking schedule for a cookout is a challenge, since everything should be ready to eat at exactly the same time. If you're serving grilled vegetables, grilled steaks, and grilled Texas toast, you've got your work cut out for you. If you intend for everything to be served at an appetizing temperature, you'll need platters and plenty of aluminum foil. (Meat will continue to cook under the foil, but the best way to keep it warm is to store it, wrapped, in a 200-degree oven.)

6. At a cookout, it's perfectly acceptable for guests to eat off paper plates and drink from plastic cups. If you're serving steaks, chops, or even chicken breasts, you'll want to furnish them with metal knives and forks.

7. Make sure the platters on which you place the cooked food are absolutely clean. **Do not** use the same dishes in which the meat marinated, particularly if you are serving chicken or pork.

8. When the cooking is done, turn off the grill. As soon as your guests are gone, scrub it with a wire brush.

Words to the Wise

Nothing is less appetizing—or more dangerous—than undercooked pork or chicken. That's why it's wisest to grill these meats over a medium flame. If it's too low, they'll dry out before they're cooked through. If it's too high, they'll burn on the outside and still be raw inside. Until you learn the intricacies of your own grill (and every grill does have its own personality), it's a good idea to cut into the pork chop or chicken breast to check the doneness. If you see any sign of pinkness, let them grill a minute or so more.

Seared Energy

Grilling continues to be popular, not only because of the special flavor it brings, but because it allows the host to cook with very little fat or oil. The following are a couple of alternatives to grilling beefsteaks and pork chops. These are not delicate fare, but they are less potentially lethal than the more traditional options.

Glazed Grilled Salmon Steaks

Yield: 4 servings

3 Tbs Dijon mustard

3 Tbs soy sauce

3 Tbs safflower oil

3 Tbs brown sugar

1 tsp prepared horseradish, well-drained

4 salmon steaks (8 oz each)

Prepare grill. (*See How to Start a Charcoal Grill on page 104*) In a medium bowl, mix together first

five ingredients for the glaze. Brush both sides of the fish with the glaze, saving a small amount for after the fish has cooked. Place the fish on the grill for 10 to 15 minutes, turning twice. The fish will begin to flake when done. Remove the fish and brush with the remaining glaze. Serve hot.

Grilled Vegetables

Yield: 4 servings

¾ cup olive oil

¼ cup balsamic vinegar

½ tsp garlic, minced

¼ tsp chopped fresh basil

¼ tsp chopped fresh oregano

¼ tsp chopped fresh tarragon

Variety of firm vegetables (squash, tomatoes, broccoli, mushrooms . . .), thickly sliced

In a medium bowl, mix the oil, vinegar, and herbs. Place the vegetables in a shallow dish (or

airtight container) and cover with the marinade. Refrigerate overnight.

Grill the vegetables on a hot grill until tender or grill marks appear. Remove from the grill and let cool to room temperature. Arrange the vegetables on a platter and sprinkle with some leftover marinade and chopped herbs.

On the Rise

Brunch for a Bunch

A brunch allows the host to entertain a good many friends in a casually elegant manner, yet it doesn't require him to take out a second mortgage. Since the standard brunch menu consists of eggs, toast, fruit, and muffins, it permits the host to spend a bit more on the champagne for the mimosas or the vodka for the Bloody Marys. Because it summons up visions of leisurely, wasted mornings that lead into languorous afternoon naps, a brunch can be an especially beautiful, even sensuous, occasion.

The Game Plan

1. Brunches seem most appropriate in colder weather, when it's too chilly to tailgate before the ball game or when you want to offer a respite from the holiday party rush. Thus, the

food needs to be satisfying, even if the portions are not huge.

2. Although a brunch should technically occur somewhere between the traditional breakfast and lunch hours, it may happen any time before 2 P.M. Before noon, the brunch menu may lean more toward eggs, waffles, and muffins. Around lunchtime, it might include smoked salmon, shrimp, or a chowder with French bread.

3. Brunches are always supposed to seem leisurely. If guests are planning to head off to a ball game or a theater matinee, give them plenty of time to enjoy their meal, have a drink, and revel in one another's company.

4. It's a simple fact of nature that dust and dirt show up more clearly in the daytime than at night. On the day before his brunch, a gentleman gives everything an extra sweep with the dust cloth, the vacuum, and the dust mop. Because there will be lots of sunshine, he does his best to make the windowpanes shine.

How to Make It Happen

1. When planning a brunch menu, the savvy host avoids serving any dish that cannot be prepared the night, or even the day, before. If he is smart, he will serve an egg casserole, a quiche, or a frittata, and avoid attempting omelets customized to each guest's individual taste.

2. Before going to bed on the night before his brunch, the host sets up the buffet table, making sure all the dishes, glasses, and serving pieces are clean.

3. Brunches always have an upscale air about them. As opposed to many other kinds of parties, they seem inherently ill-suited for plasticware and paper plates. If the host does not own enough plates and flatware, he may feel free to borrow from friends or family, of course, inviting that friend to enjoy the brunch, too.

4. Guests at a brunch will be expecting to serve themselves from a buffet, selecting

whatever seems most appealing to them, going back for seconds if they like.

5. If his brunch guests will be eating off their laps, a gentleman provides them with plenty of places to sit and plenty of flat surfaces on which to rest their plates.

6. A brunch is no place for an open bar. Champagne, white wine, screwdrivers, and Bloody Marys are the appropriate drinks. (Of course, the orange juice and the Bloody Mary mix also make nice options for nondrinkers.) Anything else is overkill.

7. As a general rule, at a brunch all the food is served at once on the buffet. However, the dessert, especially if it should be served hot, may be brought out after everyone has finished at least one serving of ham and eggs.

8. For a brunch, it's best if the background music actually stays in the background. Go for jazz or light classical music. Rock 'n' roll does not go well with scrambled eggs.

9. Because it theoretically takes the place of breakfast, brunch is one of the few times when coffee may be served along with the meal. The host may offer regular coffee as well as decaf. Throughout the party, he makes sure the pot remains full.

Words to the Wise

Brunches are leisurely affairs, but they are not intended to go on all day. Once dessert has been served, and everyone has had a final cup or two of coffee, the host, who has been up since early morning preparing for his party, may be ready for his guests to depart. He may give a hint by beginning to pick up the napkins. If he is ready for his friends to leave, he definitely stops pouring the champagne.

How to Set Up a Buffet

As a buffet allows guests to serve themselves, it must include everything they will need to enjoy their meal and must provide easy access to the food (preferably with the table in the middle of the room).

Whether the brunch table is set against the wall, the host is serving from his kitchen counter, or the table is in the middle of the room, guests will move alongside in a single line. Plates should be stacked

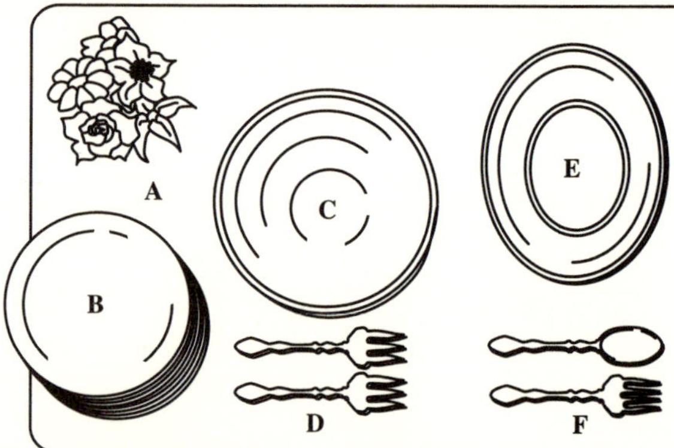

Guests begin here ➡

A. Floral Arrangement (optional)
B. Plates
C. Salad
D. Salad Utensils
E. Entrée
F. Serving Utensils
G. Side Dishes

at the beginning of the line and flatware, rolled in napkins at the end of the line, which gives guests a free hand to serve themselves.

Every dish on the buffet must be accompanied by a serving spoon or fork. Coffee, juices, and other beverages may be served from a separate table.

Flowers are a nice touch, provided they do not take up too much room. Candles can be glamorous. But don't light them. This is a brunch; that means sun is still shining outside.

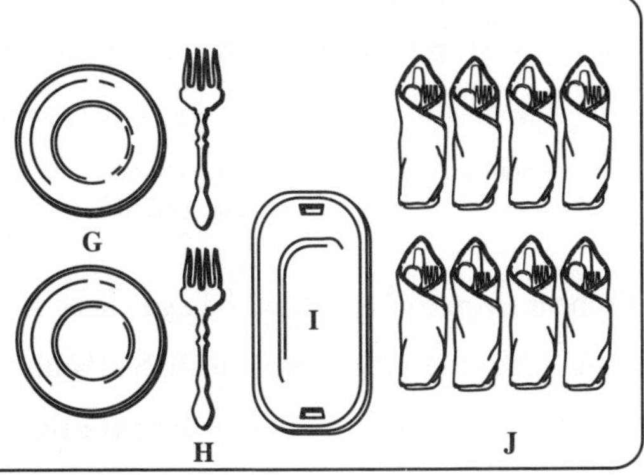

H. Serving Utensils
I. Bread Platter
J. Flatware/Napkins

Sunny Side Up

Everything about a brunch should seem unhurried. A hot dish can be prepared the day before, except for the cooking. Serve it alongside some muffins, a bowl of sliced fruit, and a tray of mimosas, and the host's job is *almost* effortless.

Egg and Sausage Casserole

Yield: 6–8 servings

6 hard-boiled eggs, sliced	1 lb hot sausage, cooked
Salt and pepper	½ cup dry bread crumbs
1½ cups sour cream	1½ cups cheddar cheese, grated

Preheat oven to 350°. Mix the egg slices and sausage in a buttered casserole dish. Salt and pepper to taste. Pour the sour cream over the eggs and sausage. In a small bowl, mix the bread crumbs and cheese, and sprinkle over the mixture. Heat in the oven until the cheese is melted.

In the Line of Duty

The Business Lunch with Clients or Coworkers

A business lunch is a curious form of hospitality. It is not intended as a time to have fun; it is a time to cut deals, plot strategies, and, if the host is lucky, impress new clients. At such times, matters of protocol and the pecking order can lead to awkward moments, unless the host has thought ahead and carefully strategized his fail-safe plan of attack.

The Game Plan

1. When setting up a meeting with clients or coworkers, the host makes sure to let them know that lunch will be part of the deal. It's embarrassing for everybody if the clients have grabbed a sandwich on the way to the host's office, thinking they would have to work through lunch.

2. When setting up a business luncheon, the host makes it clear whether business will be conducted before or after the meal is served. Business discussions may proceed during the meal, but the host should not expect his guests to pull out legal pads and take notes.

3. The host always makes a reservation when planning to take clients to a restaurant on business. If possible, he requests a quiet table where they may conduct their business in private.

4. In selecting a restaurant, the host attempts to select an establishment with a varied menu, one that offers vegetarian options, if possible. He may want to treat out-of-towners to the local fare, but not everyone may be enchanted by a plate full of fried ravioli or pulled barbecue.

5. If a gentleman plans to entertain clients or coworkers at a private club, even in this day and age, he will want to make sure that club has no membership restrictions that might offend his guests.

6. If the host plans to conduct business in a restaurant, he does not bring along cumbersome flipcharts and scale models. Such visual aids belong in a conference room. There will not be room for them among the plates and silverware.

How to Make It Happen

1. As with any other business appointment, the host arrives for his business lunch on time. (Since he is the host, he should arrive ahead of time, just to make sure his table is ready.) If he is detained, he calls the restaurant so that his guests can be assured that he is on his way.

2. The host informs the server that he and his guests will be conducting business so the server may respect their privacy. If the host and his party are on a tight schedule, he lets the server know the time at which they must be finished and ready to leave the restaurant.

3. A gentleman host turns his cell phone to the "vibrate" mode when beginning his luncheon meeting. Because he wants to give his

clients his full attention, he waits until they have departed before checking his messages.

4. If he has a chance, the host informs the server ahead of time that he will be paying the bill.

5. If the host's clients choose to order a cocktail or wine at lunch, he does not feel compelled to do the same.

6. When a gentleman has invited clients to a lunch meeting, he must pay the bill.

7. If the lunch is part of a planning session involving coworkers, the host and his associates may agree to split the bill. Keep in mind, however, not all restaurants welcome, or even allow, servers to split a tab. Be prepared to handle the situation graciously and fairly. If everyone's bill is approximately the same, the tab may be divided equally. If one guest has only had a salad, while everyone else has had pricey steaks, the host must ask each guest to pitch in whatever he or she feels is fair, including a portion of the tip.

If the host feels it is appropriate to split the tab, it is his responsibility to act as "banker" and cover any deficit.

8. If the server has done his or her job efficiently and attentively, the host makes sure the party has left an adequate tip.

9. If the host expects to be reimbursed for his lunch, he makes sure to ask for a receipt.

Words to the Wise

Not everyone likes to mix business with pleasure. A gentleman may very well want to ask his client if a lunch meeting is to the client's taste. If the client says, "I don't do lunch. Can I meet you at your office at 2:30?" the gentleman must acquiesce. He knows that, no matter what his business, most of his potential clients will not be swayed by his having picked up the tab for a meal. He invites them to lunch in order to do business, not to put them in his debt.

How to Leave a Tip

Whether he is entertaining clients at a business lunch or friends at a birthday party, tipping is a matter that concerns only the host and the server. The host does not brag about leaving a generous gratuity. If the service has been inferior, he does not inform his guests that he plans to leave a less-than-sizable tip.

To recognize good service, the host leaves at least 15 percent of his total bill. Excellent, attentive service justifies a tip of 20 percent or more. If a business lunch has dragged on for more than an hour, tying up the server's table, the host may take that situation into account when leaving his tip.

On the other hand, if the service has been minimally acceptable, the host may leave only 10 percent. If he is so dissatisfied that he feels the urge to leave less, he leaves nothing and explains his actions to the manager. Angrily leaving a dime or a quarter demonstrates that the customer and the server are equally ill-mannered.

Away from Home

Dinner in a Restaurant

Although a host may throw swell parties in his own home on a regular basis, inviting guests to dinner in a restaurant implies a special level of generosity. He can cook and slave all day in preparation for a dinner party, but nothing impresses friends, relations, or a potential lover, like a guy who's willing to order a bottle of good wine—then pick up the tab.

The Game Plan

1. There are plenty of reasons a gentleman may choose to entertain in a restaurant. He may hate cooking. He may not have enough room to entertain comfortably. He may simply want to mark a special occasion, such as a birthday, an anniversary, or a good friend's visit from out-of-town. Whatever the reason for his choosing to invite friends to a restaurant, he understands

that he is responsible for their having a good time, the same as if he were entertaining them in his own home.

2. In selecting a restaurant, the host makes sure it is one that he can afford. He also attempts to select a restaurant that his guests will enjoy. If he knows they are not meat eaters, for example, he does not drag them to a steak house. On the other hand, if they are steak lovers, he does not subject them to an establishment where the specialty is bamboo shoots and tofu.

3. When inviting his guests to dinner in a restaurant, the host makes it clear that he is paying for dinner. He may say, for example, "Paula, I hope you and Tom can join me for dinner next Friday at The Bon Vivant. I've invited Marcia and Joe, too. I'd like you all to be my guests." To make doubly sure there will be no embarrassment, he lets the server know, early on, that he will be paying the bill. Better yet, he slips his credit card to the maître d'; that way, there will be no arguing when the time comes.

4. If the restaurant dinner marks a milestone—such as a birthday or a promotion—the host makes sure everybody at the table is aware of the occasion. If he discovers that the restaurant's servers are known for their rendition of "Happy Birthday," he offers to pay them extra money to squelch their urge to sing.

How to Make It Happen

1. The host makes his reservation well ahead of time, leaving a credit card number if one is requested. He makes sure to ask the name of the person who takes his reservation, writing it down for reference, should any confusion arise on the night of his dinner party.

2. When making his reservation, the host asks if the restaurant has a dress code. If a jacket, or a jacket and tie, is required, he makes sure to inform the gentlemen in his party ahead of time.

3. The host makes every effort to arrive at the restaurant a few minutes early. That way, he can claim his reservation and make sure the table suits his tastes. He does not wait alone at the table. Instead, he goes to the bar and orders a drink, even if it is only iced tea.

4. Once all his guests have arrived, the host and his party proceed to their table. He seats them, just as he would for a dinner party in his home, splitting up couples in an effort to encourage fresh conversation.

5. For reasons of budget, or because he is familiar with the menu, when it comes time to order, the host may make suggestions.

6. If the gentleman's guests are wine drinkers, he may order for the entire party, or they may order by the glass. Ordering by the bottle, as a general rule, is cheaper, and it also allows the host to maintain control of the wine list. If he asks one of his guests to make the wine selection, he may be asking for trouble. At the same time, if the guest suggests a wine that is

out of his price range, the host may say, "That's a little rich for my blood, Gloria. What about something in the twenty-five-dollar range?"

7. If all his guests are not served at the same time, the host urges them to begin eating. Otherwise, hot food will be getting cold, and cold food will be warming up, wasting the host's money by ruining the taste of the food.

8. If there are nonsmokers in the host's party, he asks for a nonsmoking table. Smokers may feel free to step into the bar and light up whenever they choose, but nonsmokers cannot escape from a smoke-filled room.

9. It is the host's job to look out for his guests' best interests. If a guest spills her wine or drops his fork, the host does his best to attract the server's attention.

10. If the host notices that one of his guests is not touching the entrée, he encourages him or her to order another dish. If the guest declines to do so, the host drops the subject.

11. Some popular restaurants, particularly when

they are newly opened, do not take reservations. When deciding to take his party to such an establishment, the host must accept the fact that he is setting up a game of Russian roulette. If he is informed that his party will have to wait more than forty-five minutes, he suggests that they dine somewhere else. Although his guests may be in good spirits at that moment, two hours later they may be at one another's throats.

Words to the Wise

If a host encounters poor service while entertaining guests in a restaurant, he handles the situation as discreetly as possible. He asks the server, in specific terms, to rectify the problem, and if the problem persists, he asks the manager or maître d' to assign another server. Because he is a gentleman, the host knows it is not his responsibility to give the server on-the-job training. Because he is a gentleman, he would never make a scene in front of his guests.

How to Order a Bottle of Wine

When hosting a dinner in a restaurant, a gentleman may order a bottle of wine he likes or one suggested by a dinner companion, provided that he can comfortably afford it.

In general, red wine is still the wine of choice to accompany red meat, pasta dishes with tomato sauces, and most heavy entrées. White wines are usually selected to accompany fish, chicken, salads, and pasta dishes with light sauces. However, the host may feel at ease ordering any wine he likes.

The wine will be presented to the host by the server, who will show him the label. The server will then offer him the cork, so that the host can see that it is not too dry. Next, the server will pour a sip of wine in the host's glass. The host performs a quick taste test, and, if the wine passes muster, he allows the server to pour it, first for his guests, then for himself.

The server will leave the white wine in a cooler at tableside and the red wine on the table. In either case, the host may wait for the server to return to refill empty glasses, or he may take care of that duty himself.

My House Is Your House (Sort Of)

Out-of-Town Guests

It may be your idea to invite good friends for a weekend stay, or they may suggest it themselves. The excuse for the visit may be an important ball game, a major concert, or the simple fact that it's been too long since you've enjoyed one another's company. The guests may be family members or good buddies, or the visit may be charged with romantic significance. In any case, three days of entertaining even one out-of-towner can be a major challenge. At the end of the visit you may very well be exhausted. But if you organize the experience properly, you will also have that satisfied feeling of a job well done.

The Game Plan

1. As soon as you decide to invite guests, or one guest, for a weekend visit, set some clear parameters. From the outset, agree upon:

- their date of arrival. (Setting the specific time can come later.)
- the proposed length of the visit. (It isn't enough merely to say, "Come for a few days," which is little more than an open-ended invitation.)
- where the guests will be staying. (If you do not have room for them in your own place, simply ask, "Would you like me to make a reservation for you?")
- who's picking up what major expenses.

2. If you know your friends well, you'll know what they like to do. To determine the likes and dislikes of a relative stranger, however, you may have to launch a none-too-subtle investigation. Don't simply ask, "What sorts of things do you like to do?" (After all, the guests may have no idea about what's going on in your town.)

Propose some options instead: "There's a great new skating rink at the city sports center," or "The beach over at Palm Glade is really nice this time of year."

3. At the same time, give your guests the opportunity to suggest things *they* would like to do. Before bombarding them with your plan for the visit, simply ask, "Is there anything specific you'd like to do while you're here?" More than likely, the response will be, "I'm hoping to get to spend some time with you." It's the host's job to make room for that in the schedule, too.

4. As soon as you have an outline of the weekend's activities, share it with your guests. That way, they'll know what clothes to pack and what equipment to bring. They may want to know specifically whether they will need a jacket and tie.

5. If you have pets, let your guests know about them ahead of time. Some people quite simply don't get along with dogs; others are allergic to cats. If your pets tend

to be ill-spirited or uncomfortable around strangers, this weekend may be the perfect time for them to visit the kennel.

How to Make It Happen

1. Complete your preparations for the weekend before your guests arrive. Don't wait until your guests arrive to start putting clean sheets on their beds. Once they're settled in, however, you may want to ask them to accompany you on a quick run to the grocery store. That way, they can let you know, on the spot, what kind of juice and cereal they want in the morning.

2. If you have agreed to meet your guests at the airport, be on time. When it's time for them to depart, leave home early so they don't have to make a mad dash for the plane.

3. If your friends are driving themselves, make sure they have clear, accurate directions to your house or to their hotel. Make sure they have a telephone number where you may be reached.

4. Plan a schedule that is not overly harried. Your guests don't have to be rushing from event to event all weekend long. Your plans should also fit into your budget. If you can't afford to take your friends to dinner at a fine French restaurant, although it may be the hottest spot in town, take them somewhere less expensive. Their purpose in visiting is not to be impressed but to spend time with you.

5. Your guests will not expect to eat in restaurants the entire time they're visiting. Even if it is something as simple as bagels and fruit for breakfast or sandwiches for lunch, plan on feeding them at home a couple of times.

6. If there are activities that are part of your usual schedule—a jog on Saturday, church on Sunday morning—continue them while your guests are in town, provided they don't keep you away from the house for too long. Your guests have the choice of participating or staying at home. They may, in fact, enjoy the chance to have a little quiet time while you are away.

7. Build some down time into the schedule. Your guests will probably breathe a sigh of relief when you suggest, "Why don't we just hang out around the house this afternoon?"

8. If your guests offer, at some point during the weekend, to pay for a meal or drinks, let them pick up the tab. But only let it happen once. Otherwise, unless you are paying, split the tab.

9. You may want to host a small dinner party, a brunch, or a casual cocktail party while your guests are in town. This sort of gathering offers an opportunity for them to meet your friends, but it's also an activity in which they can participate. Feel free to let them help you set the table and, if they enjoy cooking, even prepare the food. Make sure, however, that you're the one doing the bulk of the work.

Words to the Wise

For all a host's good planning, weekend visits sometimes turn out to be disasters. The guests may not be feeling well or the host may have an

emergency at the office. In such cases, both the host and his guests must make the best of a bad situation. A guest who's in poor health must simply be allowed to spend some time in bed. The host who's forced to work at the office must engage another friend to take care of his guests.

Stocking the Guest Bedroom

Even if your guests are sleeping on the sleeper sofa or a futon on the living room floor, make sure they have everything necessary for a pleasant visit. Provide each of them with a couple of towels and washcloths, and let them know where the glasses and coffeemaker are stored.

Because travelers sometimes leave home in a hurry, the host will want to have on hand shampoo, soap, toothpaste, deodorant, and an extra toothbrush for his guests' convenience. It's also a nice idea to put out a few magazines or maybe a book of crossword puzzles so that your guests can occupy themselves during the quiet time you've so thoughtfully built into the weekend.

Big Bash Theory

A Full-House Cocktail Party

Some extraordinary occasions require extraordinary celebrations. You may be asked to throw a fund-raiser for charity or a political candidate. You may want to mark one of your own major birthdays. You may want to honor your parents on their golden anniversary. You may simply want to do something on a grand scale to celebrate all your friends in one fell swoop. In any case, the big party is a major undertaking. The host cannot do it alone. But it is his responsibility to make sure it is done right.

The Game Plan

1. The term "big" is relative. If you can only squeeze twenty people into your apartment, twenty people are as many as you can invite. If you are determined to entertain an army, find an appropriate location, even if it must be rented.

2. In planning this sort of event, more so than with any other, it is imperative that the host set a budget and *stick to it*. Once you start ordering balloons and talking to the caterer, expenses can get out of hand in no time. If you can't have the party of your dreams, scale back and adjust your dreams. Your guests will never know what you didn't make happen. They'll only remember what a great party you threw.

3. Decide early on how much help you will need. If you have dependable friends, ask them to help out, either by preparing some food, by running errands, or by helping you set up and clean up. If it appears that you will need to hire professionals—a caterer, a bartender, valet parkers—engage their services well ahead of time. The same advice holds true if you decide you want to hire a band.

4. Give some serious thought to the style of the party. If your goal is to be relatively formal, you'll have to come up with glass plates and silverware (probably from a party rental

company). On the other hand, you can avoid that expense by planning a menu that requires no plates and forks at all. In that case, all you need is a more-than-ample supply of cocktail napkins.

5. Plan a menu that is appropriate to your event. Unless you're offering a full-blown supper buffet, guests will only be expecting finger food. (Your invitation will, of course, let them know what they're in for.) Because the room will be packed, no matter how huge the hall, you'll want to steer away from messy foods that guests are likely to smear on one another.

6. Decide what kind of drinks you want, or can afford, to offer. A full bar can lead to considerable expense, but beer and wine, while absolutely acceptable, can help keep the cost down. In either case, if the crowd is sizable, you will not want to let them serve themselves. A bartender will save you money in the long run. He or she will also make sure the ice bucket stays full.

The Game Plan

1. Set the date early, and stick to it.

2. Invitations to a major event must go in the mail at least two weeks ahead of time to give the guests time to reply. (For a large party, RSVPs are obligatory.) The host needs to know how much food and liquor to prepare or buy.

3. A gentleman makes sure his invitation includes all the necessary information: date, time, location, what to wear, where to park. A good host also realizes that when he sets the hours for a party, he's implying certain things. A party that begins at 5:30 P.M. implies drinks and hors d'oeuvres. If the party begins at 6:30 or 7:00, the guests may expect to get supper. A party that begins after 8:30 should offer desserts and perhaps light hors d'oeuvres.

4. If you're expecting dozens of people to be parking their cars along the street, let the neighbors know ahead of time. If it appears that they may be inconvenienced in any serious way, invite them to join the party, too.

5. No matter how huge his party, a gentleman must make an effort to greet each and every one of his guests. In a large crowd, he must make a special effort to ensure loners are not left out of the fun.

6. The host is responsible—either by doing it himself or entrusting a faithful friend—for cleaning up throughout the party. Otherwise, before the party is half over, every flat surface in the house will be filled with half-empty glasses and wadded-up cocktail napkins.

7. Unless the party is a political fund-raiser or a business-related event, avoid using name tags.

8. If there is to be a special presentation during the evening, plan it well ahead of time. "Off-the-cuff" remarks tend to get off-color after the bar has been open for awhile.

9. If the party is intended to honor the host's birthday, and he does not want toasts or a round of "Happy Birthday," his wisest course is to avoid having a birthday cake.

10. Invitations to a large party should include both a starting time and an ending time. When

that time rolls around, or very shortly after, the host shuts down the bar and begins putting away the food. That late in the game, he is not giving his guests the bum's rush. He's simply indicating that the evening is drawing to a close.

Words to the Wise

The toughest part of any large-scale event is developing the guest list. No matter how generous the host intends to be, he can never invite everybody. It's helpful to set some ground rules. For example, the host may decide that he'll only invite personal friends—not coworkers or business clients—to his birthday celebration. Some bruised feelings are almost unavoidable, but at least the host can tell himself that his decisions were not entirely arbitrary.

Mass Appeal

For a large party, the food may be as elegant as you can afford to make it. Unless your guests have been invited for supper, food is not the event's focal point. This recipe, along with a cheese tray, some sliced-up tortilla wrap sandwiches, and a tray of fresh vegetables, can keep even the pickiest partier happy.

Santa Fe Salsa

Yield: 12 servings

1 cup frozen corn, thawed

1 red bell pepper, diced

1 yellow bell pepper, diced

1 red onion, diced

1 Granny Smith apple, diced

½ bunch cilantro, chopped

1 jar (8 oz) raspberry salsa

Tortilla chips

In a medium bowl, mix all the ingredients together and refrigerate for eight hours before serving. Serve with tortilla chips.

Note: Keeps two weeks in the refrigerator.

Concerning Caterers, Bartenders, and Parkers

For a large event, a good caterer can be a lifesaver. When choosing one, however, a host should ask for references, to determine the quality of the caterer's food and service. When the party is over, the host will be glad he did his research.

It is important for the host to be frank with the caterer. If the host cannot afford beef tenderloin for two hundred guests, the caterer must know this from the start. The host will be wise to ask for a contract, or some written agreement. It will come in handy when it is time to settle up.

If the caterer is providing servers or bartenders, the host should ask ahead of time if these people will expect to be tipped. (Some caterers do not encourage tipping.) For service at a large party, the host should tip each server a minimum of fifteen dollars.

In many cases, caterers provide bartenders, however if the host must hire the bartender, he should ask for references. A good bartender will be expected to set up the bar, (the host furnishes

the liquor) serve drinks throughout the length of the party, and straighten up the bar area when the party is done. Unless the host is willing to pay extra, the bartender will expect to leave at the agreed-upon time.

The host may feel free to give the bartender a tip, but the bartender must not put out a tip glass.

If the host wishes to provide valet parking, he engages a parking service well ahead of time. He needs to decide how many parkers will be needed and where the cars will be parked. The parkers must know what time they are expected, and what time they may leave. (Parkers are usually expected to stay late. When only a few cars are left, the parkers may bring them all around.)

Unlike bartenders, valet parkers should be tipped by the departing guests. The host need not tip every parker. He may, however, wish to tip the head parker for the evening.

DISASTER RELIEF

DEALING WITH THE UNEXPECTED

What to do when. . .

You burn the entrée.

Once the house is filled with smoke, or the bottom of the lasagna is burned to the consistency of shoe leather, there's no disguising the fact that the dinner is ruined. There is simply no option except to open the windows, pick up the phone, and order takeout. If there is so much smoke that the air is unbreathable, the only choice is to find a restaurant that can seat your party—even if it means everyone has to go Dutch treat.

Somebody gets sick.

Perhaps one of your guests was feeling a little queasy before the evening began, perhaps

somebody had one too many cocktails, perhaps somebody didn't tell you that he or she is allergic to walnuts or shellfish. In any case, a gentleman is concerned because one of his guests has become ill, not because the evening has been disturbed.

The host helps the guest leave the table with as little commotion as possible, then helps the guest to the bedroom or the bathroom, if necessary, and provides a damp washcloth. If the guest has become physically ill, the host may offer a clean shirt. He is wary, however, of offering medication—even familiar, over-the-counter medication—to a guest who is not feeling well.

In no case does the host leave the guest alone for any length of time. (If another guest volunteers to keep watch, the host may return to his other friends.) As soon as possible, the host makes sure that the ailing guest is given a ride home—or to the emergency room.

You come down with the flu on the day of your own dinner party.

No matter how much work he's put into the planning, no matter how long the pork chops have been marinating, no matter how much he's paid for the wine, if a gentleman is sick—particularly with an illness that has any chance of being contagious—he does not run the risk of spreading his germs among his friends.

If he has enough notice, a gentleman spreads the word about his untimely misfortune, offering to reschedule his party, if that is his intent. (If he is in really bad shape, he may want to ask a friend to help make the calls.) For his own peace of mind, the sick host asks his guests to call back and confirm that his bad news has been received.

If he is struck down at the very last minute, his only recourse may be to put a note on his front door, offering an apology for the inconvenience and asking his friends to leave him undisturbed.

In no case does a gentleman assume that his fever will break before his guests arrive. He cancels his gathering as early as he can to avoid passing along a virus and to save his guests the spectacle of watching him wipe his runny nose while carving the pot roast.

A fight breaks out.

Just because you like your friends, they will not necessarily like, or even get along with, one another. A good host attempts to remain alert to the spirit of the room. If he senses a potentially violent dispute, he does the best he can to defuse it.

He may forestall an argument by simply walking up, stepping into the conversation, and suggesting that his guests talk about something else. He also has the option of taking one guest out of the encounter by offering to introduce him to a new acquaintance. (He does *not* suggest that it is time for another drink.)

If the confrontational guests persist in

badgering one another, the host may take a firmer stance—not taking sides, but informing them that, if they insist on making a scene, they must leave. Unless one guest is more obviously at fault, the host does not choose between them. Instead, he lets both of them bear the blame for their inappropriate behavior.

After any guest has behaved in a manner that makes an evening unpleasant for others, a host may decide, with a clear conscience, never to make that person a guest again. If he is ever asked for an explanation, he gives it in simple terms: "I wish I could invite Barry to the apartment again, but I'm afraid his temper creates problems for everybody else."

Somebody shows up with two extra friends—for a seated dinner.

Whether or not an RSVP was requested, anybody who shows up with uninvited companions in tow is being unconscionably rude. If a cocktail hour has been planned, a

gentleman uses that as the opportunity to take the thoughtless guest aside and explain, without apology, that he simply has not planned to feed any extra mouths, that he does not have chairs in which to seat them, that he does not have plates on which to serve their food.

The guest may very likely counter by saying he and his friends will not eat much or that they will entertain themselves in the living room while the others sit down to dine. The host's response, then, is, "I'd prefer we didn't try that, Larry. I'm afraid it will make the others uncomfortable. I hope you'll stay for a drink, then perhaps you and your friends can come back some other time for a meal."

If, on the other hand, there really is enough food to feed the interlopers, the host may choose to welcome them. However, he has every right, at some private moment, to tell the person who brought them, "It's been fun meeting Jenny and Sarah, but I wish you'd

given me notice they were coming. I'm just lucky I bought those extra steaks."

He does not engage in this conversation in front of his other guests, either the ones who have been duly invited or the ones who have shown up unannounced.

Somebody breaks something.

Such is life in the world of entertaining. Even the best china and crystal are intended to be used, and guests—especially male guests—can get clumsy from time to time. If he is worried about cracking the family dinner plates, a host does not use them. Instead, he uses simple, attractive plates that are tougher to break and easier to replace.

If an accident occurs, the host cleans up any mess, being careful to sweep up any shards of broken glass. Then he lets the evening proceed, finding a replacement—or at the very least a substitute—for the piece that has been

destroyed. He does not turn the incident into high drama; neither does he act as if it were of absolutely no consequence, especially if the broken item was obviously an heirloom or of rare quality. He acknowledges the moment by saying, "Accidents will happen," and adds, "I hope you didn't cut yourself."

Should the butterfingered guest offer to reimburse the host, payment is staunchly refused. The guest may be thoughtful enough to include an apology as part of his thank-you note, but should he include a check, a gentleman does not cash it. He simply tells the guest, at the next opportunity, "Let's consider the little accident with the champagne glass to be past history. It was thoughtful of you to send the check, but if it's all right with you, I'll just tear it up. Sometime, you can buy me a drink."

If the guest goes so far as to purchase a piece to replace the one he has broken, the host has no option but to accept it.

You run out of food.

It can happen, especially when the hearty eaters crowd in at the front of the buffet line. (Remember Lou Grant taking *three* servings of Veal Prince Orloff at Mary's dinner party on the *Mary Tyler Moore Show*?) If the host is lucky, there will be enough salad or rolls or casserole so that everyone will at least have something to eat.

If he has enough warning, the host may at least be able to pull something out of the freezer and pop it in the microwave. If worse comes to worse, he can only hope that his guests will offer to share before they start eating. If all else fails, the host orders takeout and suggests that one of the hearty eaters make the run to pick it up.

The safest course, particularly when feeding a number of big eaters, is to put back an extra dish of the entrée so that it can be brought out before the portions grow unacceptably slim. It feels good to be able to offer seconds. At least

it feels better than not being able to offer any servings at all.

The air-conditioning breaks down.

If the host is throwing a party in the height of summer, he already has planned a menu that does not heat up the kitchen, and he has made sure to have plenty of ice. However, a walk-up apartment, or a poorly ventilated condo, can turn into a hellhole when the air-conditioning fails.

If the host has a floor fan, he uses it for his guests. He may even try borrowing a fan from his neighbors.

A lack of air-conditioning, however, is no excuse for calling it quits. (In the old days people entertained in unair-conditioned homes all the time.) Instead, the host announces that the cooling system has gone on the fritz and asks his guests simply to tough it out. If they decide to go home earlier than usual, he does have the consolation that he can then turn the fan on himself.

You realize the food on the table is virtually inedible.

Pray that if you've really screwed up, you've screwed up on the salad. That way, at the very least, the guests will have something else to eat and will not leave the table hungry.

If you've put too much cayenne in the salad dressing, the evening is not a total failure. A platter of leathery, overcooked chicken breasts, however, spells serious trouble.

This is one situation in which embarrassment is unavoidable. A gentleman admits that something has gone very, very wrong. He removes the food from the table, not just because he is embarrassed but also because an unexpected hit of hot pepper or a mouthful of stringy, dry chicken may very well send a guest into a fit of coughing—one that could result in a trip to the emergency room.

If he cannot serve the food he has prepared, a gentleman does not simply continue to fill his guests' wine glasses. Instead, he orders a pizza

or suggests that everyone head for a table at a restaurant, perhaps returning later in the evening for dessert, if he is confident that it will not be a snafu too.

Somebody steals something.

Even if the host thinks he has scrupulously prepared his guest list, he may discover, after the fact, that a thief has slipped into the mix. If he has no idea who has made off with the ashtray, the signed World Series baseball, or last month's copy of *Details*—and if he is unwilling to launch an investigation, raising suspicions among all his guests—he simply must accept the fact that he has made a poor choice in selecting his friends.

However, if he is reasonably certain of the culprit's identity—and if the stolen item is of any value, either in terms of cost or sentiment—a gentleman may justifiably attempt to retrieve his property. Without bringing others into the investigation, he may place a

phone call and say, without too much beating around the bush, "Jerry, I noticed you admiring my Mont Blanc fountain pen the other night. I'm afraid it's come up missing. Pens are an easy thing to lose, but this one is important to me. Did you see it again before you left the apartment?"

The thief then has the opportunity to figure some graceful means of returning the pen to its owner. However, if he's prone to kleptomania, it is unlikely that the stolen pen will ever find its way home. The host has at least made an attempt to straighten out the situation. He will be careful about mentioning the incident to others, but he will be fully justified in never inviting the culprit into his home again.

Even more awkward is the situation in which he actually sees a guest pocketing an ashtray. If the item is important enough to the host, he finds a discreet moment, takes the guest aside, and says, "Before you leave, Arthur, I hope you'll put the blue enamel ashtray back in its place."

Unless the item is of such great value that the host feels justified in pressing the issue, he can do little more. If the ashtray does not turn up again, he has little recourse but to strike the offending guest permanently from his guest list.

The maître d' has no record of your reservation.

In such instances, there is no point in getting into a game of one-upmanship and creating a scene in front of your guests. If the maître d' does not have a table and cannot make one available in a reasonable period of time, the host has little option except to take his business elsewhere.

He has every right to ask the restaurant staff to assist him in securing, as soon as possible, a table at a restaurant of similar quality, in a similar price range, and, if possible, in the same neighborhood. Once again, however, if the staff is not cooperative, the host does not waste time arguing. He simply asks to use the phone and does the best he can to find a table at a restaurant he knows his party will enjoy.

Many restaurants now require a credit card deposit when reservations are made. Not only does this policy protect the restaurant from no-shows, it also means that there is less chance of a reservation being simply scribbled down on a slip of paper and crammed between the pages of a notebook never to be seen again.

One final bit of advice: When making a reservation, a gentleman is well advised to ask the name of the person to whom he is speaking. That way, he can prove that he has actually spoken to an employee of the restaurant and that he is not delusional.

Your credit card is denied.

Thinking ahead and keeping scrupulous track of your credit balance can help prevent this awkward situation. But even the most scrupulous gentleman sometimes miscalculates, or his guests spend more than he anticipated, or he discovers that his credit card has expired.

There are a few options for escape, but they

all demand honesty, frankness, and the ability to maintain a cool head.

If a gentleman is entertaining in a well-run establishment, his server will find some excuse to call him away from the table before breaking the bad news. At that point, a gentleman may ask that the server try the card again. After that, he may ask directions to the nearest ATM (if his bank balance can handle the hit), excuse himself from his party, withdraw the required cash, and return as quickly as possible to settle the tab.

If that is not an option, and unless the restaurant agrees to accept a check or to let the host pay at a later date, a gentleman must simply bite the bullet, return to his table, and ask if one or more of his guests can bail him out. He does his best to minimize the unpleasantness of the transaction, and he repays the emergency loan as quickly as possible—within the next twenty-four hours, even if it means having to borrow the money from another source.

The toilet won't flush.

If you're not good at minor plumbing, you may be lucky enough to have a guest who's handy with tools.

If, after a brief attempt at correcting the situation, it appears that an emergency repair is impossible, the evening can still be saved, even if your apartment has only one bathroom. The first step is to put a sign on the toilet, explaining that it is out of order.

Then the host must transform himself into a polished diplomat, taking a close friend, or maybe two, aside and throwing himself at their mercy. "I'm afraid the plumbing is stopped up," he might say, "and I've got all this good food and drink. Do you think we could move the party over to one of your houses?"

If your guests are any kind of friends at all, one of them will pitch in and agree to be substitute host or hostess (provided, of course, that he or she is given a head start for a hasty cleanup). Clearly, this is a crisis-control situation,

and no one will expect the substitute host to be prepared for an influx of unexpected guests. Besides, they will be able to give a party for which they didn't have to purchase or cook anything, and you, of course, will insist on sticking around to help clean up.

Do *not*, under any circumstances, assume that the broken toilet will magically fix itself or that you will get through the evening without anyone knowing the commode is broken. Get your guests out of the house, as soon as possible. Otherwise, every one of them will be in line for an unfortunate, and potentially embarrassing, surprise.

The police show up, and you didn't call them.

On occasion, even the most pleasant-spirited party can get a bit rowdy—or a thoughtless guest can continue to crank up the CD player.

In such cases, an ounce of prevention beats the cure. If you live in an apartment complex

or condominium, it's the gentlemanly thing to do to keep the noise level down, especially after 10 P.M. on weeknights—and certainly as midnight approaches, even on weekends. If you're anticipating a major celebration, such as a graduation bash, a bachelor party, or a Super Bowl blowout that may last into the wee hours of the morning, it's thoughtful to alert the neighbors ahead of time and, if they're amenable, invite them to join in the fun.

If, however, you get a surprise knock on the door and your unexpected caller is flashing a badge, the wisest course of action is to remain calm, respond respectfully to any questions, and agree, without protest, to keep the volume down. If it's 3 o'clock in the morning, your party probably should be breaking up anyhow.

Do not, under any circumstances, allow your guests to become involved with your conversation with the police—unless one of your guests happens to be an experienced

attorney. In that case, you may want to let the attorney do all the talking.

In the morning—or at the next convenient opportunity—tell your neighbors you're sorry to have disturbed their evening. Make the gesture, whether you feel you've been justly or unjustly accused, and do your best to make sure it doesn't happen again. (When a gentleman changes his address, he does so of his own volition, not because he has been evicted by his landlord.)

Basic Equipment

If entertaining with frequency, stock kitchen with:

A deep-sided saucepan, with lid.

A good-sized sauté pan, with lid. (Ten-inch diameter is a great size.)

A deep pot (at least one gallon capacity), with lid, for boiling pasta or making chili.

A colander (for draining pasta and vegetables).

A roasting pan, with rack. (Most stoves come equipped with a roasting pan; it can usually be found in the drawer under the oven.)

An oven-safe casserole.

A good-quality chef's knife. A six- or eight-inch blade is good for starters, but before long the gentleman will need a paring knife and bread knife with a serrated edge.

A cutting board, preferably dishwasher-safe plastic.

A good can opener. It need not be electric.

A salad spinner.

A long-handled metal spoon and fork. A slotted spoon will come in handy, too.

Several long-handled wooden spoons. (There is no need to spend a lot for them; that way you can feel comfortable putting them in the dishwasher.)

A wire whisk.

At least three stainless steel mixing bowls, in a variety of sizes.

Two heat-resistant glass measuring cups (one for dry ingredients, one for liquids).

A cookie sheet.

A half-dozen kitchen towels and a couple of dish cloths.

A pair of heat-resistant pot holders or kitchen mitts.

If occasionally entertaining a few friends, have on hand:

At least eight old-fashioned glasses, to be used for fruit juice at breakfast or for whiskey and other on-the-rocks drinks.

At least eight double old-fashioned glasses, for mixed drinks, sodas, and iced tea.

At least eight large, multipurpose wine glasses.

At least four dinner plates that match.

At least four salad plates that look nice with the dinner plates.

At least four soup bowls.

At least four matching cups and saucers.

Flatware (probably stainless) for four, including

Four knives

Four dinner forks

Four salad forks

Four soup spoons

Four coffee spoons.

A GENTLEMAN WILL BE STOCKED WITH:

At least a half dozen heavy white cotton dinner napkins.

At least a half dozen heavy white cotton cocktail napkins.

A couple of spare packs of heavy paper cocktail napkins.

Any of these items may be purchased at a department store, or even in some large grocery stores. The staff at a good cookware store may be especially helpful in assisting the beginner who only needs the basics for his kitchen or dining table.

GLOSSARY

bake: To cook, uncovered, in an oven.

broil: To cook, in an oven, under direct, overhead heat.

buffet-style: The style of serving a meal (any meal) in which all the dishes are set out at one time—on a sideboard, a counter, or a large table—so that guests may serve themselves.

BYOB: The standard abbreviation for "Bring your own bottle" or "Bring your own booze." BYOB indicates that guests are expected to bring their own liquor or other beverages. The host is expected to provide all ice, sodas, and other mixers.

chafing dish: A serving dish, usually a heat-proof glass casserole dish, useful in keeping food warm because it is suspended by means of a metal frame over a low heat source.

china: Plates, bowls, platters, or other serving pieces made of porcelain.

cocktail: A mixed drink consisting of more than one hard liquor or wine, perhaps served over ice but not diluted by a mixer such as soda, tonic water, or fruit juice.

dishes: Plates, bowls and other tableware made from clay, glass, or even plastic. Dishes made from these materials are perfectly fine for use at any gentleman's table. However, they should not be confused with china.

family-style: The style of serving a meal (any meal) in which guests are seated around the dining table with all the dishes presented before them at one time. The guests may feel free to serve themselves or to serve one another.

flatware: The general term for all spoons, forks, and knives used at the dining table.

Heimlich maneuver: A first-aid technique used to relieve blockage of the esophagus. An invaluable skill, and one that every well-prepared host should have in his repertoire. Training in the Heimlich maneuver is

frequently offered at local chapters of the American Red Cross.

highball: A mixed drink consisting of at least one hard liquor or wine and one or more mixers, such as soda, tonic, or juice; most often served on the rocks.

hollowware: The general term used for all metal serving bowls, trays, and pitchers.

hors d'oeuvre: Bite-size food served to accompany cocktails or as a means of staving off hunger before a full meal is served. An hors d'oeuvre is served apart from the meal, while an appetizer is served as a course.

marinate: To soak meat, or sometimes vegetables, in a marinade (a liquid sometimes flavored with spices, herbs, and fruit juices). Marinating allows the flavors of the marinade to be absorbed into the meat or vegetables prior to cooking.

preheat: To turn the oven on ahead of time allowing it to reach the desired cooking temperature before food actually goes into

the oven. Most ovens have an indicator light. When the light goes off, the oven is hot enough.

RSVP: The standard abbreviation for the French phrase *Réspondez s'il vous plaît* (simply translated, "Please reply"). When a gentleman writes "RSVP" at the bottom of his invitation, he expects a reply from everyone he has invited—the ones who plan to attend *and* the ones who must turn him down.

Regrets Only: A more casual alternative to "RSVP," and a convenient option when a gentleman is hosting a large event. When a gentleman's invitation indicates "Regrets Only," he expects to hear only from those who will *not* be able to attend.

roast: To cook meat or vegetables at high heat in an oven.

sauté: To cook thinly sliced meat or, more often, vegetables in oil or butter over moderate heat.

sear: To cook quickly over an extremely high

heat in a skillet or sauté pan using very little or no oil.

silverplate: Flatware or hollowware made of base metal plated with silver.

simmer: To cook in liquid over low to moderate temperature, never reaching a full boil.

stainless: Flatware or hollowware made of stainless steel.

sterling: Flatware or hollowware made almost entirely of silver, with a small amount of copper added for strength.

stoneware: Dishes, bowls, platters, or other tableware made of clay that has been fired at an extremely high temperature, making it safe to use in the oven or at the table.

vegan: A person who abstains from eating any animal products. A vegan does not eat dairy products, eggs, or meat of any kind. In planning a dinner for vegan guests, a host may want to ask their advice in planning the menu.

vegetarian: A person who abstains from eating meat. Some vegetarians do eat seafood and/or chicken. Others eat no meat at all. Most traditional vegetarians, however, do eat milk products and will enjoy dishes that are made with cheese or other dairy products.

Vinaigrette (vi-ni-GRETT): The simple but classic French salad dressing, a mixture of vinegar, olive oil, and other seasonings. Once mastered, since it may be sweetened with honey or spiced up with pepper and onions, it is the no-fail dressing for almost any salad.